BEFORE THE FOUNDATION OF THE WORLD

EVER ASCENDING: THE RESURRECTION SERIES VOL. 3

L. Emerson Ferrell

Voice of The Light Ministries

Voice of The Light Ministries

BEFORE THE FOUNDATION OF THE WORLD
© 2017 L. Emerson Ferrell
EVER ASCENDING: THE RESURRECTION SERIES VOL. 3

Category   Reformation

Published by Voice of The Light Ministries
              P.O. Box 3418
              Ponte Vedra, Florida 32004
              www.voiceofthelight.com

Printed in   The United States of America

ISBN-10   1-933163-90-9
ISBN-13   978-1-933163-90-1

CONTENTS

WHAT YOU
WILL DISCOVER

I. WHAT IS
BEFORE THE FOUNDATION OF THE WORLD?

There are many amazing verses in the Bible, but the phrase *before the foundation of the world* spoken by Jesus and quoted by Paul, Peter and John changed me forever. I believe, if you will take the time to study this book and use it as a tool in your journey with Christ, it will do the same for you.

After I discovered the difference between the words earth and world, my perception of life was radically altered because I realized I was experiencing what I had created. Moreover, I learned to use the spiritual keys that were deposited in my spirit before creation to overcome any obstacle in the material world. This book was written to change the way you think about yourself and your future, by allowing fresh revelation to open dimensions inside of you. You are a spirit, and as such, you are living in eternity right now.

For this reason, **what** you believe and **why** is perhaps the most important principle to understand.

Believing is the most miraculous force inside of man because his beliefs ultimately determine the kind of life a man or woman will live on this earth. The freedom to choose what to believe is equally important because it separates mankind from the rest of God's creation.

Our incredible powers of belief and choice originate from a spiritual instrument called the soul and contrary to popular opinion, it is not the physical apparatus labeled the brain. The challenge for mankind is to comprehend and understand the existence of a dimension, which surrounds us daily, outside our physical realm. The next step is to depend on that realm for answers to questions regarding our origin as spiritual beings. If this book can activate your spiritual senses, you will rediscover what you knew *before the foundation of the world*.

II. WHAT JESUS MEANT BY "END TIMES"

What and why we believe the things we do determines the choices we make each day. One of the most important topics of today's modern church and the driving force for many other beliefs is what Christians call the "end times."

Regardless of your position on the subject, it will subtly influence your spiritual life because it is the number one focus of the majority of the main stream Christian Church.

Study and be eager and do your utmost to present yourself to God approved (tested by trial), a workman who has no cause to be ashamed, correctly analyzing and accurately dividing [rightly handling and skillfully teaching] the Word of Truth.

2 Timothy 2:15 AMP

Therefore, our responsibility to accurately divide the Word of God will equip us to find answers that can assist us in our search. This book will examine why this subject has contributed to many of our fears and anxieties in life.

I have told you these things, so that in Me you may have [perfect] peace and confidence. In the world you have tribulation and trials and distress and frustration; but be of good cheer [take courage; be confident, certain, undaunted]! For I have overcome the world. [I have deprived it of power to harm you and have conquered it for you.]

John 16:33 AMP

The first thing we need to settle is that Christ was victorious over the tribulations of this world and instructs those who would follow Him to live in peace because of His conquest. This was not a partial or incomplete battle, but a total triumph!

Nevertheless, over the centuries, church leaders of the various denominations have not been able to reproduce this victory and peace. This contributed to their creating doctrines and theologies to compensate for their lack of success. That is not to say that God did not miraculously visit the lives of many great men and women throughout history, like Alexander Dowie, William Branham, George Whitfield, Johnathan Edwards, Maria Woodworth-etter and Charles Finney, to name a few.

Each and every person listed above encountered The Ancient of Days in miraculous ways. Nevertheless, at the heart of these giants of the modern church was a common theological "thread" that I believe perpetuated both the "end times" doctrine and the "system" of the church we have today. The "thread" in each of their lives centered on their interpretations of the prophetic books of the Bible, especially Daniel and Revelation.

The return of Christ after a worldwide tribulation, is a central theme most Christian Churches perpetuate.

Year after year and decade after decade, men and women stand before their congregations proclaiming the imminent return of Christ during their lifetime. There have been a few who have gone so far as to give dates for this event. The result has always been the same and yet the next generation grows up hearing and believing the same dogma. Why?

I believe one of the primary reasons for the perpetuation of this belief is because God responds to faith and regardless of a person's interpretation of the scriptures, if he or she releases faith, God responds.

Therefore, people who experience miracles will also adopt the theological models of the one whom God used to change their condition, regardless if it is true or not.

Faith is a spiritual force that has nothing to do with our theology, but it has everything to do with our personal desire to meet God.

Love is the major spiritual ingredient that produces faith in a person. Once a person encounters the Love of Christ, they will desire to know Him and that will produce "child-like faith." Theology or doctrines cannot produce faith because they are a product of the soul, not of the heart.

Many people who receive outstanding miracles receive the power of God as easily as a child who responds to the love of their parents. God responds to the faith of the people. Therefore, signs and wonders have nothing to do with the theology of the person releasing faith. However, often times the new believers are contaminated with the same erroneous doctrines because of the miracles, which as we said, are not the result of doctrine, but faith.

The Bible must be understood as God's completed work to save man, otherwise, the sacrificing of His Son was in vain. The whole Bible is a prophetic book written about Christ from Genesis to Revelation. If it is interpreted from any other position, it provides a platform for the one making the interpretation to receive the glory and not God.

My purpose for this book is to provoke those who are questioning the scriptural interpretations they have been indoctrinated with over the years. I want to implore you to allow the Holy Spirit to teach you, even if it disturbs your comfortable condition of waiting on something to happen in the future.

III. DIVIDING GOD'S WORD INTO 4 SECTIONS

It has been my experience that if we divide the Bible into four sections, we are more likely to see the big picture of God's hidden strategy to trap satan and rescue man:

1. Choosing the blood line of the Messiah

2. God's long-suffering with Israel

3. The transition between the Old
   and New Covenants

4. Victorious living through the New Covenant

The first section is dedicated to the choosing of the bloodline of Abraham as the vehicle God would use to redeem man. Abraham, Isaac, and Jacob are the patriarchs Israel was supposed to model.

The second part of the Bible displays God's long-suffering and protection for Israel. The prophets warned Israel that God's judgment was coming through the Messiah, which was also prophesied to satan in the Garden of Eden.

The third part of the Bible describes in detail the end of God's covenant with Israel beginning in Daniel. This was the most tumultuous time ever on the Earth, as The Lion of Judah reclaimed His Kingdom while judging His enemies. We identify this beginning in Daniel and culminating in Revelation.

The fourth and most important part of the transition is the power to live today in the victory of Christ's completed work. Your greatest adventure begins when you experience that reality.

My desire and pursuit of Christ took me on a journey that continues to unfold beyond my wildest expectations. My life was devastated after I realized how little I knew the risen Christ.

Nevertheless, the humility to recognize my lack of knowledge positioned me to discover dimensions of Christ that I would never have found any other way. These encounters have produced a voracious appetite within me to never stop pursuing the ways of The Father.

I believe many who read this book will find new and exciting adventures with the Holy Spirit that are exactly what you have cried to know. The Spirit has been eager to show you what you knew *before the foundation of the world*. Think about that for a minute!

If we are NOT waiting on Jesus to do something, our attitude will attract the One who overcame.

If one searches the mysteries of the scriptures with this attitude, the Holy Spirit will direct them to the right places. My goal, and hopefully yours as well, is to discover Him and not another doctrine or theology. This makes me confident that our journey will not be disappointing and the direction will be "ever ascending."

SECTION I

BEFORE THE FOUNDATION OF THE WORLD

As you read this book the Holy Spirit will activate *a knowing* inside you that you have been unable to use your language to describe. These are some of the treasures that our Father placed inside your spirit *before the foundation of the world.*

Several years ago during a time of worship, the Lord opened heaven so I could see myself before time as a spirit inside of Him. His love for me was overwhelming. My mind and emotions were flooded with His love and light, which I recognized as the substance that formed my spirit. All of the communication was transmitted by visible thoughts that appeared both transparent and liquid.

I experienced an ocean of knowledge and possibilities that immersed my spirit in both joy and expectation. Everything was moving and spinning but the motion did not create any shadows or darkness, so it was impossible to measure time or speed.

The peace that passes all understanding was the atmosphere that permeated my spirit and opened my spirit to recognize my origin IN HIM *before the foundation of the world*. It was in that place that I experienced *knowledge without learning*. His love was both a light and frequency that produced all life. I knew I was created to reproduce that frequency in a physical body.

He is allowing me to share this experience to encourage those who have had or will have similar encounters with the risen Christ. I believe we all resided inside the Spirit of God before time and physical consciousness. It was there that our names were written in The Book of Life, because we all agreed to fulfill our assignments on Earth.

I knew that I had agreed to leave a mark on my generation that would resonate with a frequency that would attract others to that sound. Each one of us witnessed Jesus complete His assignment and sit at the right hand of the Father. Therefore, we all chose to run the race because we knew He had finished the work *before the foundation of the world*.

Remember, He destroyed the works of satan in order that you may finish your race in victory. Our enemies have already been defeated. Unfortunately, distractions have prevented many of you from awakening to your commitment. Be of good cheer, it's not too late to awaken and finish the course that was set for you *before the foundation of the world.*

Jesus, Paul, John, and Peter are recorded using the phrase *before the foundation of the world.* But what is even more fascinating is that each one of them is speaking about a real place and an event that occurred outside of time. Moreover, it also appears as if they were describing this experience as one who consciously observed the event. I personally believe they were present, as were you and I, if we are In Christ.

> *Father, I desire that those also, whom you have given me, may be with me where I am, to see my glory, which you have given me because you loved me* **before the foundation of the world***.*
>
> *John 17:24 NRSV*

> **Just as he chose us in Christ before the foundation of the world** *to be holy and blameless before him in love.*
>
> *Ephesians 1:4 NRSV*

He was destined before the foundation of the world, but was revealed at the end of the ages for your sake.

1 Peter 1:20 NRSV

All who dwell on the earth will worship him, (the beast) whose names have not been **written in the Book of Life** *of the Lamb slain* **from the foundation of the world**.

Revelation 13:8 NKJV

The beast that you saw was, and is not, and will ascend out of the bottomless pit and go to perdition. And those who dwell on the earth will marvel, whose names are not written in the **Book of Life from the foundation of the world**, *when they see the beast that was, and is not, and yet is.*

Revelation 17:8 NKJV

The scriptures above represent both a description of God's Kingdom and a dimension outside of time. If one tries to comprehend those verses, let alone the Bible, without that fundamental revelation, the scriptures will neither activate our spirit, nor open our understanding to remember our origin *before the foundation of the world.*

My motivation for writing this book is to provoke us, who love Jesus, by exposing us to the revelation that will help to uncover our true spiritual nature. If we allow the Holy Spirit to truly lead us through the scriptures, we will discover more than our daily bread. This will require each reader to challenge their own preconceived ideas and doctrines. If you do this, I believe you will discover your destiny that was implanted in you *before the foundation of the world.*

That may sound strange at first, but if you mediate on the reality of eternity and timelessness, your spirit will be quickened. This is necessary if you want to grasp the vastness of God and the limitation of time. This may seem daunting and a bit scary but it will force you to either trust God or continue to trust man. Paul states the position of absolute strength:

> *I am content with weaknesses, insults, hardships, persecutions, and difficulties for Christ's sake. For when I am weak, then I am strong.*
> *2 Corinthians 12:10*

I believe you are on the verge of entering into a realm of God you have never known. However, it will require a total abandonment from most of what you have been taught.

In other words, it is totally unfamiliar in your present condition, but **before** you were in this life you were *in Christ*, as Paul says in Ephesians 1:4.

One of the keys in beginning a transition outside of your current condition, as well as of time and space, is the comprehension of the words earth and world.

THE WORLD AND THE EARTH

The meaning of the words *world* and *earth* are paramount for discovering our true nature. By the time you finish reading this book, you will be well on your way to unlocking the mysteries of the Bible that previously required you to depend on others for its interpretations.

Both *world* and *earth* define different dimensions that interact with man, even though they are often used to describe both the planet we live on and our interaction with the inhabitants of the earth.

The Bible clearly explains God's creation of the physical universe, including man. This was achieved first inside of Himself and outside of time. This is important to realize if we want to understand the phrase, *before the foundation of the world*.

The Hebrew language defines the word **world** *(tebel)* as "*duration*" or "life span" and **earth** *(erets)* as dust, ground, land, or dirt.

The Bible clearly shows God as the Creator of heaven and earth, which makes Him the owner. Although God created man, He gave him the unique ability to choose whom and what to believe.

In short, the earth belongs to God, but man creates his world from his right to choose whom and what to believe.

If we explore the various uses of these words from different translations in the scriptures, the easier it will be to understand the difference between the words. All of these verses offer the reader a view of an action completed *before the foundation of the world.*

> *"For the **pillars of the earth** are the Lord's, and he **has set the world upon them.**"*
>
> *1 Samuel 2:8 NAB*

This verse in 1 Samuel describes an interaction between the earth and the world that appears to resemble the visible and invisible realms. This is just one of the many places where such a distinction is found in the Bible.

> *But if the LORD does something entirely new, and the **ground (earth)** opens its mouth and swallows them alive down into the **nether***

world, with all belonging to them, then you will know that these men have defied the LORD."

Numbers 16:30 NAB

Yet their voice goes out through all the **earth**, their sayings to the end of the **world**. Of the heavens has God made a tent for the sun,

Psalm 19:4 AMP

The **heavens and the earth** belong to you. And so does the **world with all its people because you created them.**

Psalm 89:11 CEV

Before the LORD who comes, who comes to **govern the earth**, To **govern the world** with justice and the peoples with faithfulness.

Psalm 96:13 NAB

Her feet go down to death, to the **nether world** her steps attain;
Proverbs 5:5 NAB

She will take you down to the **world of the dead**; the road she walks is the road to death.

Proverbs 5:5 TEV

He has sworn who **made the earth by His power**, *and established the* **world by His wisdom**, *and stretched out* **the heavens by His skill**.

Jeremiah 51:15 TEV

Look at this design and witness the majesty of our Creator. Man was created as the son of God, but his failure was due to the wrong use of his spirit and soul. Jesus, as the Last Adam submitted to the perfect design of listening to the Spirit and responding with His soul. The verse below illustrates this process that we all had access to *before the foundation of the world.*

I speak what I have seen with My Father, and you do what you have seen with your father.

John 8:38

The verse in Genesis perfectly illustrates the difference between *world* and *earth.*

And the Lord God formed man of the dust of the ground, and breathed into his nostrils the breath of life; and man became a living soul.

Genesis 2:7 NK

The physical body of man was produced from the dust of the earth and then he was given life from the breath of God. Life began for all mankind through the activation of man's spirit and soul with God's breath.

Man was created to have dominion in both the physical and spiritual realms. His material body was fashioned from the land he was created to rule, while his spirit was attached to His Creator for eternal life.

God supplied man with a soul, which both bridged the spiritual and material realm. The soul provided him with choice, imagination, and consciousness.

The word *consciousness* is used to describe what a human being comprehends in the present or in the "now" between the past and future.

Consciousness is an awareness of a dimension outside of time and space and one's relationship with that realm.

God gave man *free will*, or choice to create his world, but because of sin he lost his relationship with the spiritual realm.

Therefore, his perception of life and reality were limited to his soul or physical senses.

Thus, his world was formed from that limited perception. This will help us to understand what Jesus came to redeem.

> **For God loved the world** so much that he gave his only Son, so that everyone who believes in him may not die but have eternal life.
>
> John 3:16 TEV

The most famous verse in the Bible, John 3:16, makes much more sense now that we understand that Jesus died for the soul of man and not for the earth.

Our reality or "world view" is formed early in life by culture, religion, society and our five senses. The world we defend as reality is constructed from our mental images and perceptions that are built from our experiences, beliefs, media, and family.

We defend these beliefs and perceptions, in order to protect the most sacred of those images, which we identify as, ME or I. According to science, there is no place inside our physical body that can be identified as "me." That is why the term consciousness is even more difficult to describe.

God desired a being like himself who could co-create the *world* within the restrictions of the physical dimensions of time and space or **manifest His consciousness into the physical dimension**. Therefore, He created man after His image and with the power of imagination.

It was precisely the imagination of man that was perverted by Adam's sin in the Garden of Eden. The desire to worship the created instead of the Creator is the sin that separates man from God. This was the result of our having free choice, but what seemed to be a curse actually was the perfect plan of God.

The Lord saw that the wickedness of man was great in the earth, and that every imagination and intention of all human thinking was only evil continually.

Genesis 6:5 AMP

The past, present and future of everything that God created was completed inside of Him or from within the spiritual dimension before He created the physical realm. This means that inside each human being are the spiritual resources necessary to manifest heaven on earth.

The challenge each generation faces, is to decide if they have the necessary courage to really follow the Holy Spirit.

Change is never easy, nor is it comfortable and more times than not, most people will always resist it. But once you taste the goodness of Christ, you will do what is necessary to maintain that connection.

The Bible says God is the Father of all spirits, which is the means He still uses to communicate with His children. This should inspire us to become better acquainted with our original nature, in order to speak with our Father.

Once we understand that the source of all material things originated from the invisible or spiritual realm, our trust will dramatically shift from the material to the spiritual.

That is why Jesus said in Matthew 6:33, "Seek first the kingdom of God… ", but as we discover in Luke, "the Kingdom of God" is invisible.

Some Pharisees asked Jesus when the kingdom of God would come. His answer was, the kingdom of God does not come in such a way as to be seen.

No one will say, 'Look, here it is!' or, 'There it is'; because the kingdom of God is within you.

Luke 17:20-21 TEV

Do you see how critical it is to understand our spiritual origin? That is the true reality of all things that are both visible and invisible. Therefore, instead of the physical realm the spiritual dimension must be our building blocks for reality and consciousness.

In the 1960's, a large number of persons living in the United States built underground "bomb shelters" because of the fear of a nuclear attack from Russia.

The *collective consciousness* of the country believed they could protect themselves from disaster by building these bunkers. It is this *collective consciousness* that produces fear and wrong beliefs in the countries and nations today.

I believe this is the condition of the church today and it is the result of a *collective consciousness* formed from wrong doctrines and theologies. The church maintains the assumption that there will be a global destruction followed by the return of Jesus to Jerusalem to reign, even after Jesus declared that His Kingdom was in our midst as we just read.

Those who know Christ have had a **conscious encounter with Him**. Yet, if they follow the same models, which have produced this wrong *collective consciousness* in the church, they run the risk of missing their assignments given to them *before the foundation of the world*.

After we experience the reality of the risen Christ, our fundamental beliefs should be altered. We will be guided by the Holy Spirit to read the scriptures differently.

The consciousness of this world is formed from fear and doubt because that is the fruit from an evil imagination or mentality. At birth, mankind is controlled by this consciousness. **We must know this!**

> *Now there was a day when the sons of God came to present themselves before the Lord, and satan also came among them.*
> *Job 1:6*

The devil had legal authority to accuse man before God. However, the finished work on the cross by Jesus of Nazareth removed satan from power and his right to accuse us before God.

Notice, I referred to Jesus by His earthly title, Jesus of Nazareth, which is no longer His name. He is the risen Christ. This will also help you discern the difference between Jesus and the risen Christ.

The rule of satan over man ended when Jesus resurrected as the Living Christ and was crowned King of kings and Lord of lords of both the physical and invisible realms.

The majority of the inhabitants of the earth are still influenced by the sin consciousness of the "first Adam" even though Christ has liberated them.
That limits the Holy Spirit from helping people, because of their right to choose what they believe.

For example, the Bible speaks of Jesus *destroying the works of the devil*, but if persons still believe the devil has authority over them it prevents the Holy Spirit from intervening. Remember, Jesus said, "Nothing is impossible if you believe," that statement applies to both blessing and cursing. A wrong belief forms this destructive *sin consciousness* among those who love and desire Jesus.

There is no doubt that this sin consciousness from generation to generation has created spiritual strongholds in regions. The Holy Spirit will send men and women to manifest God's Kingdom over these powers and principalities. This has been called spiritual warfare, but in reality, it is manifesting in faith what was finished *before the foundation of the world*.

Deliverance is a major part of our ministry because the average church person who finds Jesus is taught a gospel message that renders people powerless to change their condition. This is because they believe Jesus must return to defeat their enemies. We must stop trusting those whose theology promotes fear and destruction.

We should start following the Holy Spirit who was sent to lead us into all truth.

If we believe Jesus needs to return to defeat the devil, then it is because we have never understood the following verse:

> Now is the **judgment of this world**; now the ruler of this world will be cast out.
> And I, if I am lifted up from **the earth**, will draw all peoples to Myself.
>
> *John 12:31-32 NKJV*

Jesus makes a distinction between the words *world* and *earth*. In fact, He describes Himself as the One who will attract His Church **IF** His completed work is elevated above the earth, outside of time and physical perception.

But on the other hand, if what He has done remains hidden on the earth because we refuse to change our sin consciousness, nothing will ever change. As we said earlier, one of the ways the truth stays hidden is by identifying the Lord as "Jesus of Nazareth," instead of the risen Christ. A sin consciousness will teach us to imagine Jesus as He was before His death and resurrection.

Those who believe a lie will not experience the freedom of what Christ fulfilled. The consciousness of the church reminds me of the story of a millionaire who died as a beggar because he refused to believe he had any money in his bank account.

God created the physical universe to serve man and to remind him of his origin and assignment. The more encounters we have with the resurrected Christ, the greater the impact will be on both our faith and consciousness, which we will later learn are one and the same.

God's Original System vs. Man's Operating System

The plan of God *before the foundation of the world* was to redeem His creation. That redemption was necessary because of Adam's transgression or separation from God. His disobedience was the sin that was passed to the human species and it was the legal right satan had to oppress man.

However, God was not surprised by Adam's sin. In reality it was part of an even greater design. (This subject is thoroughly discussed in my book *The Last Adam.*) I was taught the world was full of sinful people who cursed, drank and lied and unless Christians evangelized them with the "Gospel of Christ" most of them would go to hell.

After several encounters with Christ, I began to understand the world was different than what I was taught.

My world was the result of my thoughts, teachings, and ideas. My beliefs and actions were the result of my wrong belief, which is the same for those the church labeled as sinners.

I have since learned that man was a sinner at birth, not because of his actions, but because of his bloodline that connected him to the first Adam.

It also became obvious that my behavior would not change until my soul or mind was converted to the reality of what Christ had accomplished by His death and resurrection.

That kind of transformation required the new birth that is described in John 3. (This is the main subject of my book *Immersed In Him*.)

The brilliance and majesty of God is beyond man's comprehension and that is why He completed everything necessary to redeem man before creation. This can be extremely difficult to understand if people remain ignorant of their spiritual origin and only focus on their physical needs.

The reality of what Jesus accomplished in the physical world is more wonderful than words can describe, this is why it must be understood from the spiritual realm.

The power of this knowledge will disconnect people from past interpretations of the Bible and lead them to depend on the Holy Spirit as their Teacher, which is one of the main goals of this book.

Unfortunately, religions have an agenda that has operated most effectively by confusing people with wrong interpretations of the scriptures.

This book is not written to condemn flesh and blood, but it is a statement against the anti-Christ spirit that has captured people through a message of fear.

What God wants us to recognize and believe is that **Jesus completed His assignment, in order for the Holy Spirit to train His people.** We must be confident that God is taking us to a higher place in Christ.

We have discovered that the words *world* and *earth* do not mean the same as it pertains to the scriptures. The analogy of a computer will help that distinction become more vivid.

A computer must have hardware and software to function. The software is called the OS or operating system and without it the circuit boards, computer chips, and monitors will not work.

Visualize the *earth* as the hardware and the *world* as the operating system or software.

Let us examine the differences between the mind and brain. If we think of the **brain as the earth** and the **mind as the world** we can better understand the relationship between our body and soul. The mind has incredible abilities, but for the purposes of this analogy let us focus on the **imagination**.

The mind instantly converts thoughts into images in order to communicate it physically with the earth. The brain is responsible for both storing and manifesting the images into the physical realm. Artists, painters, and sculptors are great examples of this process. In fact, in Exodus 31:3, we find God infilling artists with His Spirit to create His tabernacle on earth. This process originated in the spiritual realm and manifested in the natural.

The knowledge to create was given to man by His Creator. Man used it to form his world and eventually that power produced his downfall. He began to worship his creation and not his Creator.

They exchange the truth about God for a lie; they worship and serve what God has created instead of the Creator himself, who is to be praised forever! Amen.

Romans 1:25 TEV

God designed man as a spirit with a soul to serve as a mediator between the spiritual and physical dimension. The soul or mind was to be a co-creator with God by the use of the imagination. The enemy knew that if he could corrupt the imagination he could severe the connection between God and man.

The world, or as we have labeled it, the Operating System (OS), was designed to function in harmony with **man's mind and brain** to create physically what he envisioned spiritually.

But man's imagination (or Operating System) was contaminated by sin whose virus has not only infected the software, but the hardware as well.

*The Lord saw that the wickedness of man was great in the earth, and that every **imagination and intention** of all human thinking was only evil continually.*

Genesis 6:5 AMP

*When the Lord smelled the pleasing odor [a scent of satisfaction to His heart], the Lord said to Himself, I will never again curse the ground because of man, **for the imagination** (the strong desire) of man's heart is evil and wicked from his youth; neither will I ever again smite and destroy every living thing, as I have done.*

Genesis 8:21 AMP

Jesus *the Christ* is the **O**riginal **S**ystem, which is why He is called *the Last Adam*. Therefore, He is the perfect anti-virus-solution that will remove our corrupted hardware and software and replace it with His Spirit.

For God loved the world so much that he gave his only Son, so that everyone who believes in him may not die but have eternal life.

John 3:16 TEV

The verse above demonstrates brilliantly that "world" and "eternity" is speaking about a dimension outside of the physical universe.

The *world* God purchased through His Son is available to those who allow Him to transform their complete system for His Original System, in order that they may enter His Kingdom.

In fact, when Jesus told people to repent and receive His Kingdom He was describing a new software and hardware that is not available to man in his current condition because of Adam's sin.

Man must be **reborn**, in order for his spirit to be controlled by God's **O**riginal **S**ystem.

> *I tell you,* **No; but unless you repent** *(***change your mind** *for the better and heartily amend your ways, with abhorrence of your past sins), you will all likewise perish and be lost eternally.*
>
> *Luke 13:5 AMP*

The mind of mankind (or his consciousness) is corrupted by sin, which has affected his physical body. The remedy requires a spiritual transformation described by Jesus to Nicodemus as being "*born again.*" Paul describes it as being a new creature, which would allow the Holy Spirit to install His **O**riginal **S**ystem that would resemble Adam before sin destroyed his hardware and software.

Man or religious solutions involve wiping the hard drive or installing programs that are neither spiritual nor effective. They leave man worse off because they don't exchange both software and hardware for God's **O**riginal **S**ystem.

In other words, they use a model or system created from the soul, such as the various self-help programs used for drug addicts, alcoholics, sex addicts and the like.

This is the method most religious systems use to try to change a person. They don't understand that the problem cannot be resolved from a corrupted soul. That is why it won't work. Man is a spiritual being and the only way he can be transformed is by the One who created him, The Spirit.

Our brain stores images or files, because to function as a human being we must have a program or system to follow, otherwise the brain shuts down. That is why man would prefer to have a priest or pastor tell him what to do.

Remember, the analogy of hardware and software? The computer will not work without an operating system (OS) or a set of instructions and files. The problem is that our entire Operating System is contaminated with a deadly virus called *sin* that has destroyed both hardware and software.

Our body and soul cannot be replaced, but they can be reborn as discussed in John 3. Therefore, the only solution is spiritual, which (in the computer analogy) requires a completely new system that we call God's **O**riginal **S**ystem.

But you must never eat from the tree of the knowledge of good and evil because when you eat from it, you will certainly die.

Genesis 2:17 GWord

The fruit which Adam consumed is what produced the virus. Adam is both the host and transmission of the virus for all the future generations of the earth. Moreover, his soul or software is the OS that is installed at birth for all the future generations.

The bloodline of man sustains the virus in both the hardware and software. Thus, the only remedy that destroys the virus is the spiritual transfusion from the Blood of Christ or the Last Adam.

A. OCCULT ORIGINATES FROM CULTURES

The consciousness of this world began from the mind or OS of Adam, which has reproduced cultures and traditions throughout the earth. These have been celebrated, accepted, and considered normal behavior. For example, celebrations arising from Easter and Christmas are nothing more than "pagan traditions."

These traditions are responsible for both hindering and perverting the move of the Spirit, in every generation.

The word "occult" originates from the word culture. The perversion of society is celebrated in the name of culture, which derives its authority by "witchcraft" and satanic worship.

Man's birth on earth makes him dependent on both the consciousness of the culture and physical perception of "reality." This means man begins to form his beliefs and realities from his surroundings. Our physical birth makes it easy to forget our spiritual origin.

The sin consciousness operates through man to infect both the physical and spiritual dimensions. Therefore, the *virus* called *sin* produces both physical and spiritual death.

Jesus is the bridge back to our original spiritual condition. However, He must be encountered through "water and the Spirit," which transforms our current condition into His image, while supplying life to our physical bodies.

Now the real work begins as we start to remove all the corrupted files that have been stored from our physical birth. **This task is impossible without the assistance of the Holy Spirit and the knowledge of the resurrected Christ.**

Jesus told Nicodemus, "one must be born of water and the Spirit" to see the invisible kingdom of God.

The earth, as well as our physical bodies, are mostly water and Jesus is also described as the Living Water.

Saturating one's self with the words of Jesus attracts the Spirit of Truth into our life, and will eventually lead us to the spiritual birth, if one never stops pursuing Him.

Over the years, people have asked me how they would know if they were "born again." I believe those types of questions arise from persons with a genuine desire to follow Christ.

However, the answer is different for each person. It would be like me asking you to describe what makes water wet?

Perhaps, the most important aspect of a New Birth for me was the power to choose the invisible realm as my source of reality.

My awakening to God's Kingdom is ever ascending and I believe that to be a common denominator with many who experience the "Water and Spirit" in the new birth.

It is my belief that each spirit made a commitment with The Father of all Spirits *before the foundation of the world*. That conversation (or *knowing*) is available to those whose spirits are rejoined to The

Spirit. Therefore, the true "evangelical message," in my opinion, is to awaken our spirits and others to that commitment through the power of the Holy Spirit.

Therefore, as we have said before and will continue to repeat throughout this book, **God created the Heavens and the Earth, but man creates the world he lives in by what he believes.**

The Holy Spirit will identify our wrong interpretations and beliefs if we continue to pursue the risen Christ. The malicious virus that was installed in the heart of our computer system at birth must be removed, but that is our responsibility.

B. YOU ARE THE WORLD GOD LOVES

For this is the way God loved the world: He gave his one and only Son, so that everyone who believes in him will not perish but have eternal life.

John 3:16 NET

The phrase "For God so loved the world," is very familiar to many people around the world. The power and depth of that verse is overlooked because most people have never considered the *world* to be any different than the *earth,* let alone do they ever imagine that we create our world from what we believe.

Most of us assume that if we can't touch, smell, taste, hear, or see something, it doesn't exist. However, we now know that *true reality* originates from the spiritual or unseen realm.

Perhaps, that is why it is so difficult to understand the Bible. The Bible is a spiritual book and as such must be understood outside the realm of our senses. That makes the task of comprehension even more complicated, especially after we discover religion was created within the framework of reason and governed by our senses.

Man has always been conscious of a supernatural God, but over the centuries some have discovered it to be a lucrative business to hide the meaning of the Bible from the common man.

This was easy to do because most men are content to be told what God says rather than to attempt to understand the Bible for themselves.

Nevertheless, Jesus made it very clear that one of His most important assignments once He returned to His Father, was to send the Holy Spirit for everyone to have access to the truth of what He had accomplished.

However, the Helper, the Holy Spirit, whom the Father will send in my name, will teach you everything.

He will remind you of everything that I have ever told you.

John 14:26 GW

God's Son demonstrated the most profound love any person will ever encounter. The power of His sacrifice is impossible to comprehend from a physical or mental perspective. But, unfortunately, religion attempts to use **a powerless denominational doctrine to convert people instead of a spiritual encounter with the resurrected Christ**.

The love Jesus provided for all mankind is available to anyone who calls on His Name. The conversion process begins immediately to change the lives of those who desire His grace and mercy.

Unfortunately, in most cases after a genuine encounter with the Holy Spirit, the convert is usually indoctrinated with theologies and doctrines that prevent their real spiritual transformation.

The Bible is a spiritual book written by and about Jesus. The challenge for those who attend church or listen to interpretations of the scriptures is **to understand that Jesus of Nazareth was both physical and spiritual. His words and actions were spiritual even though everyone could experience His person with their senses.**

46

That confusion is compounded by theologies and lies that hide the truth of what Jesus accomplished. Reasoning is not the approach to use if one wants to experience the supernatural. In fact, this was the process the Pharisees' used to crucify Jesus.

Time and time again, what begins as a love relationship with the spiritual power of Christ becomes a mental transaction with the institution of religion.

Theology and erroneous interpretations of the Bible form a huge structure that hides the very essence of the Victory of Christ.

The mind of man demands **security**, in the form of a system, which is conveniently provided by **religion**.

Jesus demonstrated the solution to man's insecurity and fear by remaining connected to His Father through the Holy Spirit.

This is the only way to overcome the fear of this world. However, this threatens the system of religion, which controls the people.

Before we became flesh we were spirits in God. Therefore, in order to be led by God, we must be reconnected to His Spirit.

His greatest gift to creation is His Son, because without Jesus fulfilling His assignment in the flesh, we would not have access to His Spirit or our Heavenly Father.

> **Let the LORD, the God of the spirits of all flesh**, *appoint someone over the congregation.*
>
> *Numbers 27:16 NAB*

The primary goal of the Holy Spirit is to awaken our spirits to both our purpose and origin. Our spirits understand the supernatural and timelessness.

We are the ones who have been hypnotized by the *malware* (*malicious software*, also commonly called *evilware*) at the core of our computer systems, which causes us to function far below our original design. We must awaken to our true nature now and remember who we were *before the foundation of the world*.

THE SPIRIT OF TRUTH

There is so much we can learn from the words and actions of Jesus, but perhaps nothing is more important than understanding that everything He said and did was because He was, is, and will ever be the *Spirit of Truth.* I remember being asked after graduating from college what I wanted to do with my life? My response was the patent cliché recited by all the baby boomers, "*find the truth.*"

Fortunately, I had attended many churches and was familiar with the Bible. I had been exposed to "The Truth" even though my learning was through a religious filter. Nevertheless, over time, my desire to know Him intensified and eventually connected me to the "power" of the resurrected Christ. The journey to know Him began from small encounters with His Spirit, which provoked me to discover for myself the reality of what He completed.

What I am sharing with you is the result of a lifetime of discovering "The Truth" through my relationship with the *Spirit of Truth*. I expect everyone who is hungry for *The Truth* to search the deeper things of the Spirit of God to discover the reality of who He is and what He has done.

> *In the beginning [before all time] was the Word (Christ), and the Word was with God, and the Word was God Himself.*
> *He was present originally with God.*

> *John 1:1-2 CEV*

In John's "gospel" we discover that both God and His Word coexisted together outside of time. Therefore, if we were all spirits **in God *before the foundation of the world***, then we were in the Word before He was made flesh.

I believe this means that our spirit had committed to serve Christ before Jesus was made flesh. Furthermore, I believe our spirits witnessed "God's Word" fulfilling His assignment even before His birth, death, and resurrection on earth.

Man sinned against God, as flesh inside of time, so it was necessary for the Word to become flesh to save man from his treason against God. **As we learned, man creates his world with his soul, which is his belief center.**

The verse below explains the condition of man as it was then as well as now.

*The Word was in the **world**, but no one knew Him, though God had made the **world** with His Word.*

John 1:10 CEV

The Creator of both the *world*, and *earth* was in both realms simultaneously, but man was unaware of it. Please meditate on that verse. John is saying, (I am paraphrasing) God was inside the "consciousness of man" or the "world" but man's mind was so dark he could not see "the light." Remember the verse in Matthew?

But if your eye is unsound, your whole body will be full of darkness. If then the very light in you [your conscience] is darkened, how dense is that darkness!

Matthew 6:23 AMP

The prevailing consciousness of the earth today is that of the First Adam and unless man experiences a conversion his consciousness will not change. This mentality (or consciousness) makes it impossible for man to recognize the "Spirit of Truth" that in reality is who all men are seeking.

Before man ever took a breath, God fulfilled His promises through the perfect work of Christ.

That included restitution for man's transgression against Him and satan's removal from authority over man's destiny.

> *It was God [personally present] in Christ, reconciling and restoring the world to favor with Himself, not counting up and holding against [men] their trespasses [but cancelling them], and committing to us the message of reconciliation (of the restoration to favor).*
>
> *2 Corinthians 5:19 AMP*

Nevertheless, our inability to live that Truth is the war we wage because we all inherited Adam's mentality and bloodline at birth.

Our warfare intensifies after we submit to Christ. This is due in large part to the influence of a helpless gospel message that misrepresents Christ's victory by teaching that Jesus must return to save His church.

If we can agree that God uses the Bible as both a spiritual and physical vehicle to manifest a victorious Christ, then it would be easier to confront our circumstances from a different perception.

The simplicity to believe that Jesus was God's physical representation of grace and mercy that destroyed the work of satan and re-established His

Kingdom on earth is hidden by erroneous interpretations of the scriptures.

However, if we remember our authority in Christ *before the foundation of the world* our fear will melt and our faith will elevate above the circumstances of the physical realm.

Christ defeated the devil and won the war, but our personal revelation of Christ is built from our individual battles that employ The Spirit of Truth.

The only weapon capable of overcoming the fears and insecurities of this world is the knowledge of Christ's victory over them.

The Bible is the visible record of His achievements, which are designed to change and provoke the next generation to greater revelations about the Son of God.

If, on the other hand, we believe each generation is waiting on the destruction of the world in order for God to intervene, then it will be impossible to understand the power Christ achieved or the scriptures themselves.

The Holy Spirit is revealing to you at this time that your freedom from everything in the material world, including death, has already been purchased for you.

The trademark of the supernatural is prophecy and its origin is the spiritual dimension. God used the spiritual language of prophecy to connect the invisible with the visible. Moreover, it is the source of faith for all those who submit to His authority and victory.

A. "THE PROPHETIC" IS CHRIST

My greatest adventure began the day the Holy Spirit introduced Himself to me. That encounter opened my spiritual eyes and ears to a dimension that changed my life and understanding of the Bible forever. The One whom I met was the Author of the Book that I had so much trouble understanding. Now He would teach me the mysteries I had longed to know and connect me with His Body.

I found myself no longer trusting others for the interpretation of the scriptures, but instead, I just waited on Him to show me or connect me with His Body. I was reminded of the conversation Jesus had with Peter when He explained that He would build His Church. The Power of Christ joining His Body made perfect sense now.

It became abundantly clear that the language most churches use to interpret the Bible does not strengthen people's faith, but rather hinders it with the fear of horrible tribulations.

I know this is not done on purpose, because the precious pastors and teachers I know love the people; however, they were indoctrinated with the same erroneous teachings as everyone else.

For example, the term *prophetic* is generally used to describe a future event that was predicted by a person who is known as a *prophet*. Of course, the event must happen for that person to maintain his title, or so you would think.

Fortunately, today's false prophets are not stoned for making wrong predictions or there would be far fewer people using that title.

Nevertheless, churches assign titles to people generally because of a letter written by Paul to the Ephesians. This is referred to as the "five-fold ministry gifts."

And He gave some [as] apostles, and some [as] prophets, and some [as] proclaimers of good news, and some [as] shepherds and teachers,
unto the perfecting of the saints, for a work of ministration, for a building up of the body of the Christ.

Ephesians 4:11-12 YLT

Unfortunately, like most things interpreted from the scriptures, it becomes a model to build a system rather than an example to be used as a spiritual guide. We must understand that the Holy Spirit is our primary instructor, not Paul or anyone else.

If we want to interpret Paul's writings, which according to Peter were difficult to understand, we need to rely on God's Spirit, not in a man-made doctrine. I suggest that all of us begin to read the words of Jesus only - until otherwise directed by The Spirit.

The power of the Bible is not in the letters of the writers, but in the substance of the Word, which is Christ. Jesus said in John 6:63, "*the Words I speak are Spirit and they are life.*"

Remember the rebuke given to Peter, who wanted to build three tabernacles on the Mountain of Transfiguration to Jesus, Moses, and Elijah?

If we form a model or system, such as a denomination after a spiritual encounter, we will hinder people from depending on The Spirit.

We do not find the Apostles anywhere in the New Testament establishing a denomination. The "gifts" spoken about in Ephesians are resident inside all those born of "water and the Spirit." (John 3:5)

The different ministries identified by Paul represent a spiritual picture of the different administrations within the Body of Christ. They are simply "job descriptions" and were not intended to divide bodies of believers over a title.

The primary purpose for the "prophetic" in the Old Testament was to announce the coming of Christ, because He is the Spirit of Prophecy. Every event leading to His birth, death and resurrection was prophesied beginning in Genesis.

*Of this salvation the prophets have inquired and searched carefully, who prophesied of the grace that would come to you, searching what, or what manner of time, **the Spirit of Christ** who was in them was indicating when He testified beforehand the sufferings of Christ and the glories that would follow.*

1 Peter 1:10-11 NKJV

*And I fell at his feet to worship him. But he said to me, "See that you do not do that! I am your fellow servant, and of your brethren who have the testimony of Jesus. Worship God! For **the testimony of Jesus is the spirit of prophecy.***

Revelation 19:10

Therefore, those who identify themselves as (or answer to) the title "prophet" must reveal the Spirit of Christ and lead us to a present-day experience with the risen Christ. Those who speak by the Spirit of Christ will open our understanding to greater and greater revelations of Christ.

Today, many operate under another spirit, which is usually intimidation, greed, and divination. **This is the result of a wrong foundational understanding of the scriptures beginning with the books of Daniel and Revelation.**

In my opinion, the wrong teachings that have prevailed for centuries to persuade the Church that Jesus did not finish what He agreed to do *before the foundation of the world,* are responsible for the hopeless and helpless condition of the Church today.

How is it possible to have faith in something in the future? A person can hope for a change in the future, but hope is not faith. Faith is formed from knowing what has been completed, not what you have been told will happen in the future. That is why it says in Hebrews 11 that *NOW faith is.*

> *NOW FAITH is the assurance (the confirmation, the title deed) of the things [we] hope for, being the proof of things [we] do not see and the conviction of their reality [faith*

perceiving as real fact what is not revealed to the senses].

Hebrews 11:1 AMP

Therefore, the "Spirit of Prophecy" (or "the testimony of Jesus") must be understood correctly if we are to rightly divide the scriptures. The Old Testament, and specifically Daniel, described His birth, death, and resurrection. God used an Angel to deliver that message to assure both its authenticity and fulfillment.

Ask yourself, what language does heaven use to communicate with us? That's right, it is indescribable.

John had to use the term "*in the Spirit*" to illustrate the difference.

*I was **in the Spirit** on the Lord's day, and I heard behind me a loud voice like a trumpet.*

Revelation 1:10

The point is this, unless our spirit is connected to His Spirit, we cannot rightly divide the Spirit of Prophecy.

Here is another question you should answer. How can a person have faith in Jesus if He had to return, at some point in history, to finish what He started?

There is a very easy test that I use every time I hear someone interpret the Bible. I ask myself if this person is building faith or fear?

Therefore, trust the Holy Spirit to teach you what He wrote and do not be tossed to and fro by every wind of doctrine. Be firmly planted on the Rock, which is the revelation of Christ Jesus.

This book will give you the keys to unlock the mystery of Christ and His finished work. Then, you will experience "His faith" to enter behind the veil to see God "face to face."

There is nothing more important in our daily life than experiencing the presence of the Holy Spirit. Each time this occurs, it reminds us of the last time we had such an encounter.

What if I told you that your conscious desire to enter His Kingdom provoked these kinds of divine interventions and that this is just the beginning of a seismic shift that will alter your consciousness forever?

As I have said many times, there is a difference between *salvation* and being "*born again.*" Those who desire to enter His kingdom must be born of His "Water and Spirit." That experience requires a conscious decision to "Know Him."

All of us are traveling this road to eternity with the hope that we are prepared for what lies ahead. That is what makes each experience so divine and addicting.

One day in the near future, this experience will never lift and you will *Be In Him*. Your spiritual eyes will open and you will know what you knew *before the foundation of the world*.

There is no formula or theology that will provide that experience. It is only your hunger and passion that will open heaven over you.

The speed of that transition will be determined by your trust in the process. Each step will require greater and greater sacrifices of what you consider valuable.

The Father wants a people in the earth who will carry a greater level of Glory than ever before. He can't release His Glory on a people with no understanding because it will destroy them. Are you ready to receive His Glory to complete your assignment? I believe you are!

B. GOD´S PROPHETIC DECLARATION

Most of us began our journey as a Christian, naïve to who we were *before the foundation of the world*.

We now know that we were spirits, in God, awaiting our birth into the earth. It was during that season that we recognized Christ as God's Word and witnessed Him as the One who Was and Is and Is to come. (Revelation 1:8) But it is only the Holy Spirit who can awaken our spirit to this reality.

After our spirits awaken, we experience a new level of faith that removes our dependence from our senses. **The success of that transition depends on a number of things, but first and foremost, it starts with recognizing what Jesus accomplished.** Without a spiritual transition man will always choose to be guided by religion over The Spirit.

The Bible is a prophetic book beginning in Genesis. The Author of the prophetic is God The Father and His Word, which is Jesus, because He is the *Spirit of Prophecy.* In addition, He is the Spirit of Truth, which makes every word spoken by Him spiritual and unshakable. (John 6:63)

God cursed the serpent in *Genesis 3* and every spirit witnessed Christ crushing the head of satan *before the foundation of the world.* That means we were "IN HIM" receiving all power to overcome before we were flesh and blood.

And I will put enmity between you and the woman, and between your offspring and her

Offspring; He will bruise and tread your head underfoot, and you will lie in wait and bruise His heel.

Genesis 3:15 AMP

The prophetic declaration made by God inside of time and recorded in Genesis 3 opened the spiritual realm to the prophetic voice of God's prophets for judgment against unrighteousness and the coming of God's Messiah.

There can be no doubt that God was prophesying to all creation that His Son would come to redeem man and crush the head of satan. God's prophecy set in motion His perfect plan over satan and death. Moreover, our Bible became the journal the Holy Spirit used to document God's greatest love story and victory.

Therefore, unless we reunite with God's Spirit to awaken each generation to their spiritual position *before the foundation of the world* nothing will change.

Perhaps, you have been taught, as I was, that the Bible prophetically speaks about the destruction of the earth and the return of Jesus as a King reigning from Jerusalem. I never questioned that doctrine until I started to search the scriptures to see if Jesus actually said that.

All I could find was Jesus speaking about His kingdom being invisible, but nowhere could I find that He would return in the flesh to sit on an earthly throne.

Some Pharisees asked Jesus when the Kingdom of God would come. His answer was, "The Kingdom of God does not come in such a way as to be seen."

> No one will say, 'Look, here it is!' or, 'There it is!'; because the Kingdom of God is within you.
>
> Luke 17:20-21 TEV

The more I searched the scriptures for the truth, the greater resistance I encountered within myself. The Holy Spirit revealed how emotionally attached to that doctrine I was, and that is when I decided to fall on the stone.

> Any man falling on this stone will be broken, but he on whom it comes down will be crushed to dust.
>
> Matthew 21:44 BBE

The day I decided to fall on "the Stone," which is Christ, was the day He began to show me great and marvelous truths that had been hidden in plain sight throughout the scriptures. This is what I am sharing with you.

The most important event to happen on earth was the birth, death, and resurrection of Christ. That was the fulfillment of the prophetic words spoken by God The Father in Genesis.

One of the primary keys to help us understand the Bible begins with the recognition of Jesus as The Passover Lamb of God. Israel's deliverance from Pharaoh was the foreshadow of what Jesus accomplished for all mankind, and this was fulfilled by Him spending *3 days and 3 nights* in the heart of the earth, exactly as He said. (For a more in-depth-study of this read my book *Who Has Bewitched You?)*

We have already discussed that one of the most profound truths of the Bible is to recognize that God completed everything He promised in the scriptures before the beginning of time. Think of that!

God made a covenant with Abraham because of his faith, but the Bible says God made a covenant with Himself.

For when God gave the promise to Abraham, since He had no one greater to swear by, He swore by Himself.

Hebrews 6:13 WEY

Remember, God and His Word are One. Thus, when Jesus committed to His assignment on earth we could say, He (The Word) and God made covenant with one another.

Therefore, God's covenant with Abraham is the same covenant Christ made with you and me *before the foundation of the world*, **IF**, like Abraham **we believe God**. (Romans 4:3)

The salvation purchased for all men requires you and I to believe it by faith, the same way Abraham believed.

The fulfillment of God's prophetic Word began in Genesis and continued throughout the scriptures. The anointed prophets in the scriptures spoke through the Spirit of Prophecy, which was Jesus, because they believed God. And I believe it was also because they remembered what they witnessed in the spiritual realm before they were flesh.

Daniel was one of those anointed by God and divinely chosen for a prophetic encounter with the angel Gabriel. That meeting awakened his spirit and physically set in motion the most dramatic chain of events ever to occur on planet earth.

The Spirit of Prophecy was coming in the flesh to prove once and for all, God is God, and Christ would fulfill the covenant He made *before the foundation of the world.*

Religion is the Origin of Wrong Teaching

Religion has always resisted the Truth. The books of Daniel and Revelation have been used to confuse, mislead, and corrupt the truth of what Jesus fulfilled. If people were taught *the Truth* and how to depend on the Holy Spirit, the business of religion would grind to a halt. This is what the Jewish leaders feared the most and one of the reasons they murdered Jesus.

Religion twists *the Scriptures.* All new converts to Christianity are taught to believe Jesus was crucified on Friday and was raised on Sunday. This is taught even though Jesus clearly tells the leaders that the only thing that proves He is the Son of God is that He will be in the earth *3 days and 3 nights.*

When the multitudes were gathering together to Him, He began to say, "This is an evil generation. It seeks after a sign. No sign will be given to it but the sign of Jonah, the prophet.

Luke 11:29 WEB

Religion controls the mind of people with fear and separation. The next step in the process of corrupting new believers is by separating Jesus from the Old Covenant, which is enhanced by starting the New Covenant with the Gospels. Of course all the Bibles make it easy to believe this, because of the way the Bible was formatted by Rome.

The Catholic religion wanted to separate themselves from the Jews, so they started a "new" religion with Jesus, beginning in Matthew. The truth is, Jesus came to fulfill the Law.

> *Do not think that I came to destroy the Law or the Prophets. I did not come to destroy but to fulfill.*
>
> *Matthew 5:17 NKJV*

The page in our Bibles that says "New Testament" is strategically located before the gospels. This may seem absolutely harmless for the new convert, but in reality it takes away who Jesus was, as the Messiah to the people of Israel.

Jesus became the New Covenant for all men as the Christ, which is why there is so much confusion surrounding His birth, death, and resurrection.

The New Covenant began at Pentecost, in 31 A.D., after the Holy Spirit was sent to lead all men into the spiritual truth of what The Christ accomplished *before the foundation of the world.*

If we read the scriptures from that position, it will become very easy to understand. **Otherwise, the Bible is turned into a historical book about Israel, instead of the spiritual door to enter and sit in heavenly places with our King.**

SECTION II

THE REVELATION
OF CHRIST

The recorded events of scripture beginning with the deception of Adam and ending with the birth, death, and resurrection of "The Last Adam" are the heart and soul to both the Bible and man's search for the truth.

Religion was never the design of God nor the purpose of Christ. In fact, Jesus came to destroy the religious system whose builder is satan. The same model of control and greed for money connects all the religions of the earth and will always crucify the Son of God. Jesus made that clear when He said, *man cannot serve God and mammon.*

We were reminded in Genesis that God would rescue man by destroying satan, which would return His Kingdom. This would come to pass, but how, when and where was hidden from man and angels alike, until God sent Gabriel to reveal the details to Daniel.

The language from heaven spoken by God's messengers continues to confound anyone who uses mental reasoning. **The Bible is a spiritual book written by the Holy Spirit making it impossible to understand without His guidance.**

Nevertheless, it is my purpose to show the reader that the Bible is not difficult to understand if you settle **one basic truth**, which is, **Jesus is the fulfillment of every promise God made including the return of His Kingdom.**

If you will read the scriptures from that perspective your understanding will increase exponentially.

The Old Covenant was the shadow of Christ in every way including the various Feasts and Holy Days.

We will discover that Jesus was born on the **feast of Tabernacles**, anointed on the **feast of Trumpets**, crucified on the **feast of Passover**, buried on the **feast of Unleavened Bread**, resurrected on the weekly Sabbath, and accepted as our propitiation for sin on the **feast of the First Fruits**.

These truths solidify Jesus as the fulfillment of the Law as He stated in Matthew 5:

Do not think that I have come to do away with the Law of Moses and the teachings of the prophets. I have not come to do away with them, but to make their teachings come true.

Matthew 5:17

"Bible scholars" and "prophets" that are interpreting the scriptures differently are actually harming themselves. They want to create a people of faith but the opposite is happening. I am not coming against flesh and blood. I know that the men and women who are promoting these false doctrines are not purposely trying to harm others.

Nevertheless, there is a spirit of anti-Christ which has always resisted God's Spirit and that is the bloodthirsty spirit that has always tried to destroy God's creation.

The perversion of God's word produces a religious people who are helpless against their circumstances because they have no understanding of their spiritual inheritance completed by Christ.

We must advance the truth of what Christ accomplished if we want to change the spiritual condition of our planet for future generations.

This will not happen overnight, but the Holy Spirit works miracles with a few as He demonstrated by the loaves and fishes in the days of Jesus.

My intention is to highlight key chapters and verses that have created the majority of confusion in both Daniel and Revelation. I have also included graphics that will help you visualize and identify specific events as they occurred in time. Please keep in mind these findings are not to become a doctrine or theology.

This book is **only a tool** to provoke you to be a student of the scriptures. Challenge **what** and **why** you believe what you do. Ask the Holy Spirit to teach you, because that is His assignment. Moreover, His greatest delight is to open our understanding to receive the greatest gift ever given to mankind.

A. DANIEL´S PROPHETIC LINEAGE

Daniel was a very special young man for many reasons, but I believe the fact that he was born into the tribe of Judah is extremely critical. (Daniel 1:6)

According to the writings of Josephus Flavius, Daniel was a kinsman of King Zedekiah the last king of Judah who was appointed by Nebuchadnezzar, and was considered evil in the eyes of God.[1] Incidentally, the name of Zedekiah meant "justice of

---

[1] *Antiquities 18.186-189 by Flavius Josephus*

God" and after eleven years of refusing to heed the prophet Jeremiah's warning his eyes were plucked out by the troops of Nebuchadnezzar.

Moreover, the bloodline of Daniel was royally connected to the House of David. This is extremely important for those who want to understand his writings, because David and all those in that bloodline were awaiting the coming Messiah. For example, David wrote several verses (Psalm 2:7-9, 16:10, 22:1, 41:9, 110:4 and 118:2) that described the death and resurrection of Jesus.

It makes perfect sense that God would use the prophetic lineage of David to complete what was established *before the foundation of the world.*

There are many scriptures that have been wrongly interpreted, which is partly responsible for the sad condition of the Church today. Indeed, the prophetic scriptures have been the ones most abused, especially as it pertains to a worldwide devastation known as the "Tribulation" or "End Times" and a future return of Christ, in the flesh. Perhaps, the Bible chapter most widely used to promote an "End Times" belief is found in Daniel 9 and it has been called the 70th Week.

Daniel is one of the most powerful books ever written because it announces to all the powers and principalities that God's declaration to satan, in the

Garden, was coming to pass. His days were coming to a close because the head crusher was coming in the form of the Messiah. The clock started in the Garden but the reality of the event started *before the foundation of the world.*

You may recall that Daniel's interpretation of King Nebuchadnezzar's dream concerning the kingdoms of Babylon, Persia, Greece, and Rome described the end of the era or kingdoms on the earth. This corresponds with the reality that God was reestablishing His Kingdom that would have no end.

> *And in the days of these kings the God of heaven will set up a kingdom which, shall never be destroyed; and the kingdom shall not be left to other people; it shall break in pieces and consume all these kingdoms, and it shall stand forever.*

> *Daniel 2:44*

That verse alone removes the need for something else to happen in the future to establish God's Kingdom.

As we said earlier, God used His prophets to announce the events before they happened, in order for man to recognize the spiritual authority of God. The interpretation of the prophetic scriptures is always a challenge if one relies on anything but the Spirit.

The language of heaven is not discernable in the words of this world. Therefore, one must allow the Holy Spirit to interpret phrases like "a day is like a thousand years" or to understand the day-for-a-year principle defined in (Numbers 14:34; Ezekiel 4:6).

> *And when you have completed them, lie again on your right side; then you shall bear the iniquity of the house of Judah forty days. **I have laid on you a day for each year.***
>
> *Ezekiel 4:6 NKJV*

If we are unfamiliar with the spiritual language of heaven we will resort to using logic for our interpretations, which results in confusion and or false doctrines. Therefore, our goal is to allow the Holy Spirit to retrain us from the perspective of God's finished work announced in the Garden of Eden.

B. THE SEVENTY WEEKS PROPHESIED TO DANIEL

Know therefore and understand, that from the going forth of the command to restore and

> *build Jerusalem until Messiah the Prince,
> there shall be seven weeks and sixty-two
> weeks;*

Daniel 9:25a

Most of those who believe in the "end times" use the 70th week as their foundation. The teaching most often promoted in churches advocate that God has postponed the 70th week in Daniel 9, to allow the physical state of Israel to accept Christ as their Messiah.

This teaching essentially negates Christ's victory over the devil. In addition, it makes God a liar because of His promise to satan in the Garden.

The truth is, if religious doctrines can convince people to wait on future events, it becomes much more easy for the kingdom of darkness to control people with all kinds of false teachings. The most blatant example of this is the crucifixion on Friday and resurrection on Sunday.[2]

In essence our observation of that tradition is tantamount to our choosing to believe a religious ritual over the words of Christ. We must ask ourselves how many other religious lies have we chosen to believe instead of the truth?

---

[2] *For further information concerning that subject read my book "Who Has Bewitched You?"*

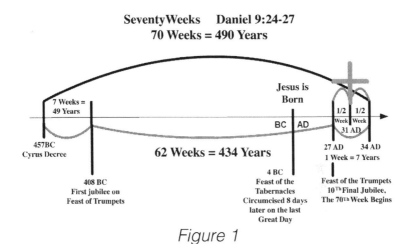

Figure 1

7 Weeks: Rebuilding of the Temple

62 Weeks: From finishing of the Temple
to Jesus being anointed

70th Week: 3.5 years of Jesus ministry,
(crucifixion, resurrection & ascension)
3.5 years to Stephen's death

The verses from Daniel 9:24-27 are being copied from the Septuagint, which was the first Greek translation of the Hebrew Old Testament.

*Seventy weeks have been determined upon thy people, and upon the holy city, for **sin to be ended**, and to **seal up transgressions**, and to **blot out the iniquities, and to make atonement for iniquities**, and to **bring in***

everlasting righteousness, *and to* ***seal the vision and the prophet***, *and to* ***anoint the Most Holy***.

Daniel 9:24

There can be no doubt that Jesus is the person being represented in Daniel 9:24. The Messiah is the only one capable of meeting the criteria listed below.

- Ends Sin
- Seals up Transgression
- Blots out Iniquities
- Bring in Everlasting Righteousness
- Seals up Vision and Prophecy
- Anointing the Most Holy

This verse in Daniel clearly describes God's Messiah. Each of the highlighted sections illustrates what Jesus fulfilled. If we examine the wording correctly, there can be no doubt that Jesus completed His assignment and left nothing undone. The most significant statement in that verse, that unites scriptures of Daniel with Revelation, is the phrase *seals up the vision and the prophet*. Look at the verse in Revelation.

And I saw in the right hand of Him who sat on the throne a scroll written inside and on the back, sealed with seven seals.

Revelation 5:1 NKJV

The *Spirit of Prophecy*, Jesus, opens the words sealed in Daniel 483 years or 69 weeks later in Revelation 5. He was the only One capable of opening the scroll and releasing the final judgment.

The graphic (Figure 1 on page 81) allows us to see the linear progression of the 70 Weeks. However, to fully understand the majestic wisdom and perfection of God *before the foundation of the world,* we have to comprehend God's Feasts and Jubilees, which were all shadows of the Christ.

THE FEASTS

I. THE FEAST OF TRUMPETS AND JUBILEE

The Old Testament Feasts and celebrations were the prophetic shadow of the One to come, whom is the substance of all things. The words of Gabriel spoken to Daniel must be understood from the perspective of the Jewish Laws, especially the Feasts and Holidays.

One of the greatest celebrations was the Jubilee that was observed every 49 years or 7 weeks. This was the freedom from all debts, captivity and slavery, which obviously described their Messiah and is recorded in both Isaiah 61 and Luke 4. The 10th and final Jubilee occurred during the feast of Trumpets in 27 A.D. when Jesus stood up in the synagogue to read Isaiah.

The Spirit of the Lord God is upon Me because the Lord has anointed Me to preach good tidings to the poor; He has sent Me to heal the brokenhearted, to proclaim liberty to the captives, and the opening of the prison to those who are bound ...

Isaiah 61:1

But let's begin from the beginning of the prophecy with the first Jubilee that occurred in 457 B.C. The sequence of events begins with a decree from King Cyrus after Israel was in Babylon for 70 years.

Thousands of exiles left Babylon to rebuild the Temple in Jerusalem. The work started in the midst of great distress and opposition; nevertheless, God protected them to assure His word would come to pass.

The restoration of the temple is described in the book of Ezra as beginning during the seventh month. It is important to note that Israel celebrates several feasts during that month.

Zerubbabel and Joshua the High Priest built the altar on the Temple mount, in order to allow the daily sacrifices to commence. This was the celebration called the **feast of Tabernacles** followed 10 days later by the **feast of Trumpets**, which was the 1st of the 10 jubilees.

And when the seventh month was come, and the children of Israel were in the cities, the people gathered themselves together as one man to Jerusalem.

Then stood up Jeshua the son of Jozadak, and his brethren the priests, and Zerubbabel the son of Shealtiel, and his brethren, and builded the altar of the God of Israel, to offer burnt offerings thereon, as it is written in the Law of Moses the man of God.

And they set the altar upon its base; for fear was upon them because of the peoples of the countries: and they offered burnt offerings thereon unto Jehovah, even burnt-offerings morning and evening.

And they kept the feast of tabernacles, as it is written, and offered the daily burnt offerings by number, according to the ordinance, as the duty of every day required;

And afterward the continual burnt-offering, and the offerings of the new moons, and of all the set feasts of Jehovah that were consecrated, and of every one that willingly offered a freewill-offering unto Jehovah.

From the first day of the seventh month began they to offer burnt offerings unto Jehovah: but the foundation of the temple of Jehovah was not yet laid.

Ezra 3:1-6 ASV

The feast of Trumpets, 49 years later in 408 B.C., announced the beginning of the 2nd Jubilee. This both concluded the first 7 weeks and fulfilled the words in Daniel 9:

And thou shalt know and understand, that from the going forth of the command for the answer and for the building of Jerusalem until **Christ the prince there shall be seven weeks**, *and sixty-two weeks; and then the time shall return, and the street shall be built, and the wall, and the times shall be exhausted.*

Daniel 9:25

The following graph depicts the picture of the first 7 weeks or 49 years. The first jubilee had come to a close with the rebuilding of the temple and the walls of the city.

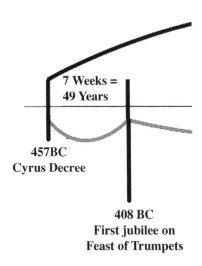

Figure 2

For the next 62 weeks or 434 years, 8 more Jubilees would occur before the Messiah would appear, according to the words spoken to Daniel by Gabriel. The prophet *Amos* describes this long period of time as the *"famine of hearing the words of the Lord."* (*Amos 8:11*)

Now fast-forward to 27 A.D. or 434 years later to the 10th and final Jubilee. Israel would celebrate the **feast of Trumpets** unaware that their Messiah was on the earth.

The power of the prophetic is God's invisible masterpiece created outside of time and space *before the foundation of the world.*

Man's world and history are filled with erroneous information and data. But God's Word is immune from that because man did not create it.

Therefore, all of us can be impacted with His Glory regardless of our level of knowledge because it is timeless and perfect.

I said that to say this, Daniel's words are rock solid on so many different levels. The angel sent from God to Daniel verifies the reality of Christ, beginning with His birth, death, end of the Old Covenant and His Kingdom without end. In addition, it unlocks our divine connection with God's love story written to you and me before time.

The Bible is both the final authority and historically perfect as our spiritual plumb line for truth. God fulfilled His word with His Word. Is it any wonder why Daniel and Revelation are the most contentious books in the Bible?

II. Historical Facts that Identify Jesus' Day of Birth and the Beginning of His Ministry

I believe it will be helpful here to use my previous book to highlight historical events in scripture that illuminate the pinpoint accuracy of God's prophetic word. The following excerpts are taken from the book "Who Has Bewitched You?"[3]

---

[3] Who Has Bewitched You?, L. Emerson Ferrell, Resurrection Volume 2. Pages 85-89

A. THE DECREE OF ARTAXERXES

In the seventh year of Artaxerxes, king of Persia, a decree was made to rebuild Jerusalem (Ezra 7). It followed the decree of Cyrus, in which he acknowledged that the LORD God of Heaven had charged him to build Him a house at Jerusalem, which is in Judah (Ezra 1:2). Artaxerxes' decree was significant because of a prophecy revealed to Daniel.

Daniel states:

Know therefore and understand, that from the going forth of the commandment to restore and to build Jerusalem unto the Messiah the Prince shall be seven weeks, and threescore and two weeks: the street shall be built again, and the wall, even in troublous times.
Daniel 9:25

This shows that there are 62 weeks + 7 weeks = 69 prophetic weeks (or 483 years).
Applying the *"a-day-for-a-year-principle"* (*Numbers 14:34; Ezekiel 4:6*), we arrive at 483 years from the decree until the beginning of Christ's ministry.

The decree was made during the seventh year of Artaxerxes' reign (457 B.C.). This date is historically well documented. By subtracting 457 from 483, we come to the year A.D. 26.

When counting from B.C. to A.D., astronomers correctly add one year since there is no year "zero", while historians and chronologists generally neglect to do this.

Adding one year brings us to A.D. 27 — the prophesied year of the beginning of the ministry of the Messiah.

Luke 3:23 tells us: "*And Jesus Himself began to be about thirty years of age...*". The context of this verse is after John the Baptist had begun his ministry and just before Jesus began His. Since Jesus was 30 years old in A.D. 27, **He would have been born in 4 B.C.**

Remember, we must add one year to compensate for no "zero-year." Thus, advancing 30 years from 4 B.C. brings us to A.D. 27.

This leads us to the next historical proof that further confirms when Christ was born.

B. THE TIME OF HEROD'S DEATH

Shortly after Christ's birth, an angel warned Joseph in a dream that he and his wife Mary were to take the child and flee into Egypt.
They stayed there until the death of Herod (Matthew 2:15). Christ was an infant less than one year of age when Herod died.

Matthew shows that:

"Herod slew all the children that were in Bethlehem and, all the coast thereof, from two years old and under, according to the time which he had diligently inquired of the wise men."

Matthew 2:16

To better establish the exact time of Herod's death, we find in Josephus' Antiquities of the Jews a reference to a lunar eclipse. A footnote in the *Whiston translation of Josephus* states:

"This eclipse of the moon (which is the only eclipse mentioned by Josephus) is of greatest consequence for the determination of the time for the death of Herod... and for the birth and entire chronology of Jesus Christ.

It happened March 13th, in the year of the Julian period [*] 4710, and the 4th year before the Christian era."
(Bk. XVII, ch. vi, sec. 4). According to Josephus, Herod died the following year, 3 B.C.

(*) Julian period, chronological system now used chiefly by astronomers and based on the consecutive numbering of days from Jan. 1, 4713 B.C. Not to be confused with the Julian calendar, the Julian period was proposed by the scholar Joseph Justus Scaliger in 1583 and named by him for his father, Julius Caesar Scaliger.

Soon after Herod's death, the angel instructed Joseph to return to the land of Israel with Mary and Jesus, who would have been about one year old.

C. TIME OF CONSTRUCTION OF THE TEMPLE

As mentioned, Christ was 30 years old (Luke 3:23) when He began His ministry in 27 A.D. Now, we will see how the chronology of the temple harmonizes with the chronology of Christ:

"Then answered the Jews and said unto Him, What sign show You unto us, seeing that You do these things? Jesus answered and said unto them, Destroy this temple, and in three days I will raise it up. Then said the Jews, Forty and six years was this temple in building, and will You rear it up in three days? But He spoke of the temple of His body."

John 2:18-21

This occurred on the first Passover during Christ's ministry, in 28 A.D. The Jews said that the temple had been under construction for 46 years. By adding one year to compensate for no "zero-year" this means that the temple's construction began in 19 B.C., the 18th year of Herod's reign.

In "**Antiquities**", Josephus wrote, *"And now Herod, in the eighteenth year of his reign... undertook a very great work, that is to build of himself the temple of God..."* (Bk. XV, ch. xi, sec. 1). The reconstruction of the Temple began in 19 B.C., which was the 18th year of Herod's reign. If we advance 46 years from 19 B.C. we arrive at 28 A.D., which was the first Passover Jesus attended in His ministry.

D. THE REIGN OF EMPEROR TIBERIUS

The time of John the Baptist's ministry provides further historical proof. In Luke 3:1 we find, *Now in the fifteenth year of the rule of Tiberius Caesar, Pontius Pilate being ruler of Judaea, and Herod being king of Galilee...*

Historians such as Josephus confirms that the reign of Roman Emperor Tiberius began about 11 or 12 A.D., since he reigned concurrently with Augustus Caesar for about 2 years.

If we add the 15 years of Tiberius' reign to 11 or 12 A.D., we arrive at 26 or 27 A.D. The account in Luke describes the time John began, which was just before Jesus came on the scene to be baptized by John in 27 A.D.

E. THE GOVERNORSHIP
OF PONTIUS PILATE

Historians agree that Pilate ruled for ten years. *Luke 3:1* shows that during the 15th year of Tiberius' reign, Pilate was governor. Some historical accounts, such as the Encyclopedia Britannica, date Pilate's rule from A.D. 26 to 36.

When he was recalled, he immediately sought help from his close political ally, Emperor Tiberius. Yet, while Pilate was en route to confer with him, Tiberius died, in A.D. 37. With Tiberius' death, Pilate's rule ended the same year. Therefore, Pilate's ten-year rule would have had to coincide with the years A.D. 27 to 37[**]

--

(**)*http://rcg.org/articles/ccwnof.html# © 2015 The Restored Church of God.*

Pilate's governorship over Judea began in early A.D. 27, during the 15th year of Tiberius' rule. Meanwhile, John the Baptist began his ministry in early A.D. 27, which preceded Christ's ministry by several months.

Jesus was born in the autumn of 4 B.C., most likely on September 29th, which was the **feast of Tabernacles** and was circumcised 8 days after on the **Last Great Day**.

Luke records that the public ministry of Jesus began during the 15th year of the reign of Tiberius. Historical and secular evidence indicate Jesus began His ministry, in the fall of 27 A.D., of the seventh month, which would be the **feast of Trumpets**.

Jesus died in 31 A.D. on the **feast of Passover**, which was on the 14th day of Nisan. This was the 1st month in the Jewish calendar. He ministered for three and one-half years.

If one counted backwards from the last feast of Trumpets in 27 A.D. to the first Jubilee you would arrive at the year 457 B.C. This would be the 10th day of the seventh month or the feast of Trumpets. This was the time Joshua and Zerubbabel finished building the altar. Israel had not sacrificed to God in 70 years because of their captivity in Babylon.

There are no accidents with God. Jesus began His ministry 27 A.D. on the feast of Trumpets. He was both God's sacrifice and altar for all mankind.

There are many who have been taught or believe that Jesus must return to fulfill all the feasts. We are demonstrating to you that God did not leave anything undone including the Feasts, which were only the shadow of the true Light:

- Jesus was born during the feast of Tabernacles

- He started His Ministry on the feast of the Trumpets

- He died on Passover

- He was buried on the feast of Unleavened Bread[4]

- He ascended to the Father on the feast of First Fruits

- He sent the Holy Spirit on the feast of Pentecost[5]

- He stood up in heaven on the Day of Atonement to receive both Stephen and all who would die in His name

---

[4] *Who Has Bewitched You? by L. Emerson Ferrell, Page 127*
[5] *Who Has Bewitched You? by L. Emerson Ferrell, Page 127*

DANIEL 9:26-27

The 70th week is the prophetic golden key that unlocked the riches of God's glory and fulfilled His prophecy to satan in Genesis 3:14-15. That is exactly why the enemy has blinded so many from the reality of the words the Archangel Gabriel spoke to Daniel.

The following two verses in Daniel 9 describe both the final week of the 70th week prophecy and the beginning of God's new covenant. Verses 26 and 27 are simple to understand if we remember that God had prophesied from the beginning to crush the head of satan and redeem man.

Most Bible teachers agree that 69 of the 70 weeks prophecy in Daniel chapter 9 have been fulfilled. The false interpretations begin with the 70th week. The picture of Jesus and what He did is highlighted in the verses and outlined below:

*And after the sixty-two weeks, **the anointed
one** shall be destroyed, and there is **no
judgment in him**: and he shall destroy the city
and the sanctuary with **the prince that is
coming**: they shall be **cut off with a flood**, and
to the end of the war which is rapidly
completed he shall appoint to desolations.*

Daniel 9:26 Septuagint Translation

There can be no doubt that each of the highlighted
phrases is a description of Jesus. Perhaps you were
told that the "prince" that is coming refers to an
anti-Christ, but if we recognize that Jesus fulfilled His
earthly assignment to become the resurrected Christ
or Prince of Peace, the verse has a different
meaning.

- *The anointed one*

- *No judgment in him*

- *The prince that is coming*

- ***Cut off with a flood*** *(I will discuss this later)*

It is very interesting to note that Verse 26 describes
the future of Jerusalem and those who refuse to
receive Jesus as their Messiah. This should not
confuse the reader because they correspond with
John's vision in Revelation where he describes the

final judgment of Israel, which happened between the years 66½ A.D. till 73 A.D.

Daniel describes these events as *time of trouble never seen before* and Jeremiah refers to it as *Jacobs's trouble.* The writings of the historian Flavius Josephus vividly describes that time in history. In his book, "*The Wars of the Jews*" he describes the Jewish Civil War that ended in the destruction of Jerusalem in 70 A.D.

I suggest that every person with any doubt about those events should read the book written by my wife Ana M. Ferrell, "*The End of An Era*", for a detailed look at that period of time.

Most Christians are unfamiliar with the annihilation of Jerusalem under General Titus of Rome, who later became Emperor. The sad truth is, over 1.1 million Jews died between 66 and 73 A.D.

At this point, you must ask yourself why the Church rarely mentions this subject? Perhaps, if more people knew the history during that time it would eliminate the false "end times gospel" being promoted in the church today.

Verse 27 corresponds to the first 3.5 years of the last 7 years. This is one of the most important times in history because it was the transition from the Old to New Covenant.

*And **one week shall establish the covenant with many**: and in the midst of the week **my sacrifice and drink offering** shall be taken away: and on the temple the abomination of desolations; and **at the end of time** an end shall be put to the desolation.*

Daniel 9:27 Septuagint Translation

• *One week shall establish the covenant **with many**.*

Verse 27 offers a complete picture of the end of the Old Covenant and the beginning of the New. God is returning the Kingdom to man through "The Last Adam." The transition is being made between the Old and New Covenant.

Moreover, and just as important, the prophecy God spoke to the serpent in the Garden of Eden was taking place in hell. Jesus was holding the keys of death and hell while crushing the head of satan. The following verse in Hebrews describes that transition.

*For then He would have had to suffer repeatedly since **the foundation of the world**. But as it is, He has appeared once for all **at the end of the ages to put away sin by the sacrifice of Himself**.*

Hebrews 9:26

These verses complete the first part of the prophecy given to Daniel 500 years earlier. God is precise! Can anyone doubt that our Heavenly Father would leave anything undone?

Nevertheless, it would require the full 7 years to destroy the abomination that left Israel "desolate."

That period of time is highlighted historically and prophetically in Revelation and in the writings of Paul.

In the midst of the week my sacrifice and drink offering shall be taken away.

Daniel 9:27

Verse 27 is very important to comprehend if we want to experience the fullness of our New Covenant.

Jesus was crucified on Passover Day, Nisan 14, 31 A.D., which was both the middle of the calendar week and the half-way point of the last 7 years in the 70 weeks prophecy.

The feast of Passover originated as God's exclusive redemption plan for the Jews. It was the greatest feast and celebrated Israel's exodus out of Egypt.

Jesus had to fulfill every jot and tittle of the Law to satisfy God's redemption plan for mankind. The crucifixion of Jesus, which was on Passover, fulfilled God's requirement for all mankind.

Jesus tells His disciples at the last supper;

> *I will never again take the produce of the vine till that day when I shall drink the new wine with you in My Father's Kingdom.*

> *Matthew 26:29*

The "Drink Offering" was a part of the "Wave Sheaf Offering" and was to be observed only when Israel entered the "Promised Land." After Jesus resurrected He had to present Himself as the "drink offering and first fruits" to His Father.

Therefore, one of the most important parts of the transition to the New Covenant required Jesus to be both accepted as the "Wave Sheaf Offering", and "Drink Offering."

This sheaf is called the "sheaf of the first fruits" or the "**Wave Sheaf**" and it was brought to the priest and offered before God as the "First Fruits" offering. If it was accepted, God blessed the harvests of those who kept His Law.

The word "sheaf" is translated from the Hebrew word "omer", which means *a measurement of about 3.5 pecks of flour.* The flour was made from beating the wheat into grain and then grinding it to flour. This was considered the **Wave Sheaf** or **First Fruit** offering.

The cutting of the sheaf took place after 6 pm on the second Sabbath of the feast of Passover and was offered in the Temple on Sunday. According to The Tanakh (Jewish Bible) the word for wave is "elevate."

> *He (the priest) shall* **elevate** *the sheaf before the Lord for acceptance in your behalf; the priest shall* **elevate** *it on the day after the Sabbath. On the day that you* **elevate** *the sheaf, you shall offer as a burnt offering to the Lord a lamb of the first year without blemish.*
>
> *Leviticus 23:11-12*

The evidence that Jesus fulfilled the **Wave Sheaf Offering** begins with the conversation with Mary and verified in 1 Corinthians 15:20. In addition, it was 3.5 days since His death, which is the exact amount of flour used in the offering.

Jesus satisfied fully both the Wave Sheaf and Drink Offering because He is both The 7th Day spoken of in Hebrews and our entrance into His Kingdom, which is the "Promised Land."

In other words, He is our *Promised Land, 7th Day of Rest* and *King of kings.*

> *For we who have believed do enter into rest, as he said, As I have sworn in my wrath, if they shall enter into my rest: although the works were finished **from the foundation of the world.***

> Hebrews 4:3 WEB

The Father accepted Jesus as the first of the First Fruits written about by Paul in 1 Corinthians 15:20-23, which means the sacrifice and drink offering would no longer be received by God.

> *Because Jesus Christ did what God wanted Him to do, we are all purified from sin by the offering that He made of His own body once and for all.*
> *Every Jewish priest performs his services every day and offers the same sacrifices many times; but these sacrifices can never take away sins.*
> *Christ, however, offered one sacrifice for sins, an offering that is effective forever, and then He sat down at the right side of God.*

> Hebrews 10:10-12 TEV

AT THE END OF THE AGES

*He then would have had to suffer often **since the foundation of the world***; *but now, once at **the end of the ages**, He has appeared to put away sin by the sacrifice of Himself.*

Hebrews 9:26 NKJV

The statement "At the end of the ages" describes perfectly what happened *before the foundation of the world*. Jesus was the Passover Lamb slain to fulfill all of God's requirements to redeem man.

The writer of *Hebrews* clearly explains that Jesus fulfilled the necessary conditions of God to justify mankind's forgiveness and to authorize satan's removal and condemnation.

There is no other "end times" and we need to understand that this is both a distraction and a deception.

We have to separate ourselves from this and reject the anti-Christ spirit behind it, lest we become responsible for the millions we deceive by it.

70ᵀᴴ WEEK FULFILLED

A. THE END OF TIMES

Daniel's life was spared because of his interpretation of King Nebuchadnezzar's dream some 500 years before Jesus.

As you looked, a stone was cut out by no human hand, and it struck the image on its feet of iron and clay, and broke them in pieces.

Then the iron, the clay, the bronze, the silver, and the gold, all together were broken in pieces, and became like the chaff of the summer threshing floors; and the wind carried them away, so that not a trace of them could be found. But the stone that struck the image became a great mountain and filled the whole earth.

Daniel 2:34-35 ESV

These verses make perfect sense if we believe Jesus fulfilled His assignment *before the foundation of the world.*

History confirms that Rome was the final worldwide empire to rule the earth. Most theologians identify Jesus as the "Stone" that both destroys the image and becomes the mountain. Nevertheless, those who promote an "end times philosophy" must create a resurrection of a new Roman Empire, to justify their false interpretation.

Our being familiar with that historical period is paramount to interpreting the scriptures of Daniel and Revelation, as well as recognizing that God's language is spiritual.

Most confusion arises if one tries to relate modern day circumstances to the events that happened in 1 A.D. The spiritual importance of the Bible is not limited to the fulfillment of the Bible in that time period. On the contrary, it is the door that will open your spiritual understanding to the reality *before the foundation of the world.*

In other words, even though Jesus fulfilled the prophetic scriptures in the 1st century, that knowledge should empower your faith to new levels.

The knowledge of what Jesus finished is the power that opens the spiritual portals over our

lives. Moreover, it will create an eternal relationship with Truth.

There are many interpretations of both Daniel and Revelation, which have been used to promote an "end time scenario." However, if you identify Christ in the language and symbolism of each verse, you will recognize the fulfillment of God's promise to crush satan's head with His "heel bruiser."(Genesis 3:15)

After reading prophecy from the understanding that Jesus fulfilled His earthly assignment, all of the fear associated with future tribulation and mayhem will disappear.

The majority of information and references used concerning this subject are from various resources. Many have been compiled from writers such as Edward L. Bromfield, Tertullian, Clement of Alexandria, Eusebius and Flavius Josephus.

All of the various writers and materials provoked me to research the information and ask the Holy Spirit for guidance and direction. If you will do the same it will greatly enhance your search for the truth.

My purpose for writing this book is to provoke you, the reader, to contend for a personal revelation of Christ. Christ is alive and extending an invitation to know Him in His majestic Glory.

Please do not exchange one theology for another. If you are investing in the time to read this book, then I am convinced the Lord will give you greater insight for the future generations.

If you will purposely look for Him through each major event in the Bible, the Holy Spirit will reveal Him to you. My prayer is that this book will serve you in that endeavor.

Graphic Pictures of the Final Week

B. 7 YEARS

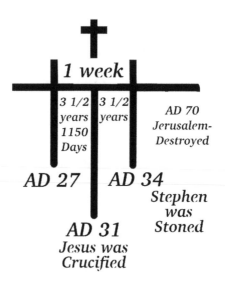

Figure 3

One of the ways to identify the last 7 years or the last week in the 70 weeks is revealed in the 1,260, 1,290 and 1,335 days mentioned in Daniel and Revelation.[6]

The graphs will serve as visual pictures of the scriptures and will illustrate the strategic placement of the feasts that represented the shadow of the coming Christ. The feasts reveal God's absolute perfection in plain sight and His desire to save Israel with their Messiah.

C. THE 1,260 DAYS

This number of days is equivalent to 3.5 years, and is also mentioned in a symbolic way as "*a time, times, and a half a time.*"

And I heard the man clothed in linen, who was above the waters of the river, when he held up his right and his left hand toward the heavens and swore by Him Who lives forever

---

[6] *Revelation 11:3 And I will give power to my two witnesses, and they will prophesy one thousand two hundred and sixty days, clothed in sackcloth. Revelation 12:6 Then the woman fled into the wilderness, where she has a place prepared by God, that they should feed her there one thousand two hundred and sixty days.*
Daniel 12:11 And from the time that the daily sacrifice is taken away, and the abomination of desolation is set up, there shall be one thousand two hundred and ninety days.
Daniel 12:12 Blessed is he who waits, and comes to the one thousand three hundred and thirty-five days.

that it shall be for **a time, times, and a half a time [or three and one-half years]***; and when they have made an* **end of shattering and crushing the power of the holy people***, all these things* **shall be finished***.*

Daniel 12:7 AMP

The Jews are those described as "holy people" in this verse and it says they were being crushed. Remember, the words of God to satan in the Garden? The Christ was crushing the head of the serpent?

The Jews were not satan, but the priesthood had been corrupted to the point that even Jesus levels the following accusation against them: "*You are from your father, the devil.*"[7] In Revelation He refers to these corrupted leaders as being from the Synagogue of satan.

> *Behold, I will make those of the synagogue of satan who say that they are Jews and are not, but lie—behold, I will make them come and bow down before your feet, and they will learn that I have loved you.*
>
> *Revelation 3:9*

---

[7] *John 8:44 You are of your father the devil, and the desires of your father you want to do. He was a murderer from the beginning, and does not stand in the truth, because there is no truth in him. When he speaks a lie, he speaks from his own resources, for he is a liar and the father of it.*

We are starting to see the way God knits His prophetic word beginning in Genesis and culminating in both Daniel and Revelation. Additionally, we discover that the book of Revelation describes both the events of the last 7 years, as well as the tumultuous transition between the Old and New Covenants. During that time, history records the martyrdom of God's disciples and the death of hundreds of thousands of Jews.

We can be the generation that refuses to be indoctrinated with the lies of the "end times philosophy" with a thorough understanding of both historical and spiritual times. For example, 3.5 is both a spiritual number and a historical time period that is most significant. It was during this time that Jesus, the *Son of Man,* became *The Christ.*

The number 3.5 is spiritually significant on many levels; it was the length of time Jesus ministered and it was the number of years that The "*woman clothed with the sun*" (The Church) was protected in the wilderness.[8]

The Gentiles tread the holy city for 3.5 years and the beast is given authority for 3.5 years. God uses the natural realm to validate the spiritual realm, in order to open the hearts and minds of people.

---

[8] *Revelation 12:6 Then the woman fled into the wilderness, where she has a place prepared by God, that they should feed her there one thousand two hundred and sixty days.*

In order to understand the three and one half years written in Daniel 12:7, we should be familiar with the calendar used during that time in conjunction with the Feasts in Leviticus.

The chart below illustrates the 13-month "*Intercalary Calendar*" used by the Jews to celebrate their feasts and holy days. Nisan is the first month in this Calendar, which God established after Israel left Egypt. That month starts in the middle of our March. The Feasts were divided into the spring and fall. The Spring Feasts celebrated Passover or Unleavened Bread, First Fruits and Pentecost. The moon determined the feasts times, which is why the calendar had 13 months and either 29 or 30 days.

YEAR	27AD	28AD	29 AD	30 AD	31 AD	Total
MONTH						
1st		30	30	30	14th day of Nisan or Passover Day	
2nd		29	29	29		
3rd		30	30	30		
4th		29	29	29		
5th		30	30	30		
6th		29	29	29		
7th Last Great Day 22nd 8 days left		30	30	30		
8th	29	29	29	29		
9th	30	30	30	30		
10th	29	29	29	29		
11th	30	30	30	30		
12th	29	29	29	29		
13th		29				
Totals	155 days	383 days	354 days	354 days	14	1260 days

Figure 4

This particular chart (Figure 4) defines the 1,260 days that begin on The Last Great Day and finish on Nisan 14 or Passover.

The fall feasts celebrated Tabernacles, Trumpets, and the Day of Atonement. **The Last Great Day was celebrated on the 8th day of Tabernacles in the month of September**, which is illustrated as the 7th month in this graphic.

Remember, Jesus began His ministry during the month of September because The Law required a Rabbi to be 30 years old and His birthday was on the feast of Tabernacles.

However, I believe He officially began His ministry during the feast of Trumpets when He read from Isaiah 61 and became our Jubilee. The Jews celebrated The Last Great Day on the 8th day of the feast of Tabernacles, which is the beginning of the 1260 days that culminates with His death on Nissan 14.

Figure 5

If we count backward 1,260 days from the 14th of Nisan 31 A.D. the day Jesus was crucified, we will arrive at the Last Great Day in 27 A.D., which is celebrated as a Sabbath on the 8th day of feast of Tabernacles.

I do not believe this was an accident because this was the day Jesus was both named and circumcised. You will recall according to Jewish custom, the male child was named the day he was circumcised and it was on that day He was called the "Son of Man." In my opinion, that is significant because satan deceived Adam. Thus, God crushed his head with the "Son of Man" or The Last Adam.

Both of the "1,260 and 1,290 days" recorded in Daniel and Revelation began during the Fall Feasts, which was the month of September. All of the Feasts in the fall season (Feast of Trumpets, Atonement, and Tabernacles) played a significant role in the last 7 years of the 70 weeks.

Please keep in mind that all of these specific days, **1,260, 1,290** and **1,335** mentioned in Daniel and Revelation highlight important events during the spiritual transition from the old to new covenants. The power of these days falling within the Jewish feasts is not by coincidence.

The revelation of the "two witnesses" in Revelation 11 is also contained within the framework of the 1,260 days. Remember, without the spiritual understanding of Christ, the Bible, as a spiritual book is impossible to understand.

D. THE 1,260 DAYS AND THE TWO WITNESSES

All of the prophetic books in the Bible declared the coming of the Messiah. But perhaps there is no other book that reveals the manifestation of the prophetic than the book of Revelation.

John's account of Jesus of Nazareth to The Christ is more easily understood if we recognize Christ as *the Spirit of Prophecy*. That realization allows the mysteries of the Bible to be revealed through His birth, death, and resurrection.

The correct interpretation of the Bible is always challenged by preconceived ideas and theologies. We must be conscious of that as we approach foundational subjects that we have assumed were correctly portrayed. The only way to prevent this from happening is to make a concerted effort to look at scripture with the foundational understanding that the work was finished *before the foundation of the world*.

The 11th chapter of the book of Revelation begins with an angel measuring what God considers holy, which are His Temple, altar and worshippers. This is an illustration of the way Jesus fulfills the Law.

The following verses reinforce the picture of Jesus completing His assignment.

I will allow my two witnesses who wear sackcloth to speak what God has revealed. **They will speak for 1,260 days**.

These witnesses are the two olive trees and the two lamp stands standing in the presence of the Lord of the earth.

If anyone wants to hurt them, fire comes out of the witnesses' mouths and burns up their enemies. If anyone wants to hurt them, he must be killed the same way.

These witnesses have authority to shut the sky in order to keep rain from falling during the time they speak what God has revealed. They have authority to turn water into blood and to strike the earth with any plague as often as they want.

When the witnesses finish their testimony, the beast, which comes from the bottomless pit, will fight them, conquer them, and kill them.

Their dead bodies will lie on the street of the important city where their Lord was crucified. The spiritual names of **that city are Sodom and Egypt**.

For 3 ½ days *some members of the people, tribes, languages, and nations will look at the witnesses' dead bodies and will not allow anyone to bury them.*

Revelation 11:3-9 GW

We discovered the ministry of Jesus lasted 1,260 days and He was both The Spirit of Prophecy and The Fulfillment of the Law. If we open our understanding we will recognize the two witnesses as the picture of Jesus.

Keep in mind the book of Revelation is not a chronological book but rather a spiritual picture that reveals, The Christ in His Glory. Many of the scenes that John records pertain to this timeless realm.

And their dead bodies will lie in the street of the great city, which **spiritually is called Sodom and Egypt**, *where also our Lord was crucified.*

Revelation 11:8 GW

Notice that there is a spiritual city called Sodom and Egypt located over the natural city of Jerusalem. Jesus referred to this city as the one that killed the prophets from Abel to Zachariah. He also stated that it was impossible that a prophet would die outside of Jerusalem.

That on you may come all the righteous blood shed on the earth, from the blood of righteous Abel to the blood of Zechariah, son of Berechiah, whom you murdered between the temple and the altar.

Matthew 23:25

Nevertheless I must journey today, tomorrow, and the day following; for it cannot be that a prophet should perish outside of Jerusalem.

Luke 13:33

We immediately recognize this to be a spiritual city because there was no such city during the time of Abel. In addition, we know this is the same spiritual city that crucified our Lord *before the foundation of the world.* Later on I will illustrate in greater detail the meaning of Sodom and Egypt.

Most theologians teach that these two witnesses are Elijah and Moses, who are killed by a person called the anti-Christ in Jerusalem. This is taught to occur either during or before a planet wide tribulation. This is contrary to the scriptures because of the verse in Hebrews.

And as it is appointed for men to die once, but after this the judgment,

Hebrews 9:27

We discovered that the 1,260 days describe the time Jesus started and finished His ministry on earth. But what does 3.5 days represent?

Jesus was in the tomb *3 days and 3 nights,* but the Law required the first fruit to be offered on the first day following the 2nd Sabbath of the Passover. The First Fruit Offering sacrifice sanctified the harvest and started the clock towards the next feast called Pentecost.

If you are not familiar with the feast of Passover and the two Sabbaths during that feast, do consult my book *Who has Bewitched You?*

Remember, the Jewish day during that time began and ended at sundown. The Wave Sheaf Offering (or First Fruits) occurred on Nisan 18 in 31 A.D., which is the day most churches wrongly celebrate His resurrection. Therefore, the morning sacrifice was at least 12 hours after Jesus resurrected on Sunday making it 3.5 days.

The description of the two witnesses illustrates perfectly that the ministry of Jesus was both the fulfillment of the Law and The Spirit of Prophecy.

The transfiguration of Jesus also demonstrates that the Law and Prophets were fulfilled in Him. Revelation 11 describes both the ministry of Moses and Elijah or the Law and Prophets.

Now we see the scripture in Matthew 5 in a totally different light!

> *Do not think that I have come to do away with or undo the Law or the Prophets; I have come not to do away with or undo but to complete and fulfill them.*

> *Matthew 5:17*

Armed with that knowledge I began to look at other translations that describe that event in Revelation 11.

It did not take long to find discrepancies in the older texts as it related to the description of "dead bodies and graves."

The Coptic and ANDREAS manuscripts[9] use the singular tense when describing "their corpse" and "grave" instead of the plural used by most modern translations. That would seem to indicate the two are really one.

> *And their dead bodies will lie in the street of the great city, which spiritually is called Sodom and Egypt, where also our Lord was crucified.*

> *Revelation 11:8 GW*

---

[9] *http://www.biblestudytools.com/commentaries/jamieson-fausset-brown/revelation/revelation-11.html*

Revelation 11:8 in our Bibles read *dead bodies*, but A, B, C, the oldest manuscripts, and the Coptic read the singular, "dead body."[10]

One of the signs Moses performed in Egypt was changing the water to blood.

> *And the Lord said, Say to Aaron, Let the rod in your hand be stretched out over the waters of Egypt, and over the rivers and the streams and the pools, and over every stretch of water, so that they may be turned to blood; and there will be blood through all the land of Egypt, in vessels of wood and in vessels of stone.*
>
> *Exodus 7:19 HSCB*

You will also recall that water and blood flowed from the side of Jesus on the cross.

> *But one of the soldiers pierced His side with a spear, and at once blood and water came out.*
>
> *John 19:34 HSCB*

Moreover, it was the prayer of Elijah that prevented rain for 3.5 years in Israel. There is that 3.5 number again.

---

[10] *http://www.sacred-texts.com/bib/cmt/jfb/rev011.htm*

But I say to you, there were certainly many widows in Israel in Elijah's days, when the sky was shut up for three years and six months while a great famine came over all the land.

Luke 4:25 HCSB

Remember this verse in the Law?

The one condemned to die is to be executed on the testimony of two or three witnesses. *No one is to be executed on the testimony of a single witness.*

Deuteronomy 17:6 HCSB

Moreover, if we recognize that God is using the Law to condemn satan it makes further sense that He would use 2 witnesses (My book *The Last Adam* explains this in greater detail). Further proof is found in the same Coptic Manuscript that describes that after His ministry He was killed by the anti-Christ spirit or beast that operated in conjunction with Rome and the corrupt priesthood of the Jews.

*When **the witness finish His testimony**, the beast, which comes from the bottomless pit, will fight **him**, conquer **him**, and kill **him**.*

Revelation 11:7 Coptic Andreas Manuscript

The 1,260 days is the 3.5-year period God used both prophetically and physically to describe the transition between the Old and New Covenants.

E. THE 1,260 DAYS IN REVELATION 12

Another powerful prophetic sign, which perfectly depicts the 70th week of Daniel, is found in Revelation 12.

John describes a magnificent display in heaven. The whole firmament is shown as a sign in the stars of both the ascension of Jesus and the removal of satan and his followers from heaven.

And she gave birth to a son, a male child, who was to have rule over all the nations with a rod of iron: and her child was taken up to God and to his high seat.

*And the woman went in flight to the wasteland, **where she has a place made ready by God**, so that there they may give her **food a thousand, two hundred and sixty days**.*

And there was war in heaven: Michael and his angels going out to the fight with the dragon; and the dragon and his angels made war,

And they were overcome, and there was no place for them in heaven.

And the great dragon was forced down, the old snake, who is named the Evil One and Satan, by whom all the earth is turned from the right way; **he was forced down to the earth, and his angels were forced down with him.**

Revelation 12:5-9 BBE

This time period in Revelation 12 describes God nourishing or protecting the "woman" or "church" on earth and Michael removing satan and his angels from heaven.

Jesus announced to the disciples what He witnessed *before the foundation of the world* and that these events would occur in their lifetime. The verses below clearly show that satan was being removed from heaven during the 1,260 days that Jesus was fulfilling His assignment.

At this moment the world is in crisis. Now satan, the ruler of this world, will be thrown out.

John 12:31 The Message

Jesus said to them, I watched satan fall from heaven like lightning.

Luke 10:18 GW

The closer we examine John's writings in Revelation the easier it is to identify the risen Christ as the purpose of the book. It was this unveiling of The Christ that both exposed and condemned the anti-Christ spirit that controlled the priesthood. John identifies the "beast" as that corrupted Jewish priesthood.

There is compelling evidence, in my opinion, that Revelation is the first book of the New Covenant, especially if one understands the history during that time.

The following verses in Revelation 12 further illustrate the period of warfare that was happening in heaven and earth during this time. The book of Daniel speaks about a flood that I believe is also recorded by John in Revelation 12.

*And to the woman were given two wings of a great eagle, that she might fly into the wilderness, into her place, where she is nourished for **a time, and times, and half a time**, from the face of the serpent.*

And the serpent cast out of his mouth water as a flood after the woman, that he might cause her to be carried away of the flood.

*And the earth helped the woman, and the earth opened her mouth, and swallowed up the **flood**, which the dragon cast out of his mouth.*

*And the dragon was wroth with the woman, and went to make war with the remnant of her seed, which **keep the commandments of God, and have the testimony of Jesus Christ.***

Revelation 12:14-17 KJV

Here is the verse in Daniel that corresponds with the vision John writes in Revelation.

*And after the sixty-two weeks, the anointed one shall be destroyed, and there is no judgment in him: and he shall destroy the city and the sanctuary with the prince that is coming: **they shall be cut off with a flood**, and to the end of the war which is rapidly completed he shall appoint the city to desolations.*

Daniel 9:26 Septuagint Translation

I believe this verse in Daniel describes the flood from the dragon whose purpose was to kill the "Child" which is The Christ. You will recall the devil, or dragon, used Herod to try to kill Jesus after His birth.

But God used the earth to protect Him for 1,260 days and His Church for 1,290 days.

The following prayer by Jesus illustrates the protection God provided during this most critical time on earth.

> *While I was with them, (my disciples) I kept them safe by the power of your name, the name you gave me. I protected them, and not one of them was lost, except the man who was bound to be lost—so that the scripture might come true.*
>
> *John 17:12 TEV*

The birth of the Church through the death and resurrection of Christ was not only prophesied 5 centuries earlier, but also protected by God. He will always protect both His Church and Word because God made covenant with His Word *before the foundation of the world.*

F. THE 1,290 DAYS

Now let´s look at the 1,290 days recorded in Daniel to further understand the fulfillment of the 70th week.

> *And from the time that the daily sacrifice is taken away, and the **abomination of desolation** is set up, there shall be **one thousand two hundred and ninety days.***
>
> *Daniel 12:11 NKJV*

The use of numbers in the scriptures frame the prophetic timetable God used to establish what happened *before the foundation of the world*. The prophetic is a tool to aid us in our journey to recognize and confirm our Heavenly Father's nature and faithfulness.

We can trust His Word because He made it flesh to fulfill every promise He made through Him.

If you discover Christ throughout the scriptures there will be no need to look for any future event to validate your experience with the risen Christ. You will obtain your spiritual authority through the knowledge of what He completed *before the foundation of the world*.

That may sound unbelievable to you, but that is because we have all been so conditioned to this finite world that we have forgotten our spiritual origin in Him before we were created. This understanding allows us to look at both our life and that of Jesus as the fulfillment of God's Word.

There are two key events in Daniel 12:11 that identify and form the 1,290-day period. Each number of days is divided between specific events and memorials or feast days. In this particular period the time was divided between the death of Jesus and the abomination of desolation.

*"And from the time that the **daily sacrifice is taken away**, and the **abomination of desolation** is set up,".*

This verse reiterates what was written in Daniel 9:27: *.. And one week shall establish the covenant with many: and in the midst of the week **my sacrifice and drink-offering shall be taken away...**"*

We have established that Jesus was crucified on Passover, Nisan 14, which was the middle of the week in the year 31 A.D. We also learned in the previous section about the specific requirement of the Law called the Wave Sheaf Offering, which occurred the first day following the second Sabbath of the Passover, which was the 8th day of the feast.

Let's take another look at this specific requirement that blessed the spring harvest and started the 50-day countdown to Pentecost.

1. THE WAVE SHEAF OFFERING

When you come into the land that the LORD is giving you and you harvest your grain, take the first sheaf to the priest.
He shall present it as a special offering to the LORD, so that you may be accepted. The priest shall present it the day after the Sabbath.

Leviticus 23:10-11 TEV

The Israelites reaped the first of their harvest after the Sabbath following Passover. If there happened to be back-to-back Sabbaths that week, they would have to wait till after the second Sabbath because they could not work (harvest) on either Sabbath.

This day was very important to the Israelites because if God accepted their offering, they would enjoy a season of prosperity from the land. In addition, it was the start of the fifty days leading to the next feast called Pentecost.

From the day after the Sabbath, the day you brought the sheaf of the wave offering, count off seven full weeks. Count off fifty days up to the day after the seventh Sabbath and then present an offering of new grain to the Lord.

Leviticus 23:15 TEV

According to Unger's Bible Dictionary, the Wave Sheaf Offering, which occurred during the 8th day of the Passover feast, marked the beginning of the harvest season for the year. It consisted of an ephah or omer of grain, which was approximately 3.5 pecks. There is the number 3.5 again.

As we learned earlier, the Omer of flour was taken to the Priest to be offered to God during the morning sacrifice. God honored the faith behind the offerings and as a result, blessed their harvests.

The Wave Sheaf Offering depicts the resurrected Christ being offered to God, as the First Fruits of the harvest of mankind.

> *But now Christ is risen from the dead, and has become the first fruits of those who have fallen asleep.*
>
> *1 Corinthians 15:20*

Jesus arose on the weekly Sabbath, which was Nisan 17, 31 A.D. The following day, Sunday was another Holy Day called the Wave Sheaf Offering spoken of in Leviticus.

> *Do not cling to me, said Jesus, for I have not yet ascended to the Father. But take this message to my brethren: I am ascending to my Father and your Father, to my God and your God.*
>
> *John 20:17 WEY*

This was why He told Mary not to touch Him before He could present Himself as the HOLY WAVE OFFERING for all mankind. He was accepted by His Father and was declared the "First Fruits" from the dead.

After The Father accepted His offering, all men would have access to Him and His perfect sacrifice.

His fulfillment of this part of The Law was what eliminated the need for sacrifice any longer.

Jesus as our spotless Lamb fulfilled The Law, which rendered future sacrifices of animal's null and void.

Fifty days later He would pour out His Spirit on all flesh as declared in Joel.

> And it shall come to pass afterward That I will pour out My Spirit on all flesh;
> Your sons and your daughters shall prophesy, Your old men shall dream dreams, Your young men shall see visions.

> *Joel 2:28*

2. THE ABOMINATION THAT MAKES DESOLATE

Our key to interpreting the 1,290 days in Daniel 12 is to identify the two events highlighted as the "***daily sacrifice removed**, and the **abomination of desolation**."*

We just identified Jesus as fulfilling The Law as our Passover Lamb. Therefore, the 1,290-day countdown begins there. But what event was considered the abomination that made them desolate? This is a serious indictment that requires our understanding of the history of Israel beginning with the Exodus from Egypt.

Within a matter of days after the miraculous crossing of the Red Sea, the children of Israel had made a golden calf to worship instead of trusting the God of Abraham, whom Moses was meeting with on Mount Sinai.

Then, throughout their history, it was revealed that they would sin, repent, and cry out to God for mercy. They would submit to God's Law for a season, but sooner or later they would return to worshipping the idols of other nations invoking the wrath of God. This behavior earned them the name of "stiff necked people."

For I know thy rebellion, and thy **stiff neck***: behold, while I am yet alive with you this day, ye have been rebellious against the Lord; and how much more after my death?*

Deuteronomy 31:27

Lift not up your horn on high: speak not with a **stiff neck***.*

Psalms 75:5

But they obeyed not, neither inclined their ear, but made their **neck stiff***, that they might not hear, nor receive instruction.*

Jeremiah 17:23

God told Solomon at the dedication of the Temple that if they rebelled from Him by following after idols that He would make them desolate. The word *shamem*[11] is the Hebrew word for *desolate*, which means *astonishment of the people who see it.*

> *But if you turn away from following Me, you or your children, and will not keep My commandments and My statutes which I have set before you but go and serve other gods and worship them,*

> *Then I will cut off Israel from the land I have given them, and this house I have hallowed for My Name (renown) I will cast from My sight. And Israel shall be a proverb and a byword among all the peoples.*

> *This house shall become a heap of ruins; every passerby shall be* **astonished** *and shall hiss [with surprise] and say, Why has the Lord done thus to this land and to this house?*

> *Then they will answer, Because they forsook the Lord their God, Who brought their fathers out of the land of Egypt, and have laid hold of other gods and have worshiped and served them; therefore the Lord has brought on them all this evil.*

> *1 Kings 9:6-9 AMP*

---

[11] *Strong's Concordance H8074*

You recall that in the prophecy of Daniel there were 1,290 days from the end of the sacrifices to the abomination of desolation.

> And from the time that the daily sacrifice is taken away, and the **abomination of desolation** is set up, there shall be **one thousand two hundred and ninety days**.
>
> Daniel 12:11 NKJV

It was just after Stephen quoted Psalms 102, and Leviticus 26:41, that he was killed.

> Heaven is My throne, says the Lord, and the earth is my footstool. What kind of house would you build for me? Where is the place for me to live in?
>
> Acts 7:49 & Psalm 102:25

> **Ye stiff-necked and uncircumcised in heart and ears, ye do always resist the Holy Ghost: as your fathers did, so do ye.**
>
> **Acts 7:51 & Leviticus 26:41**

God promised Solomon that His judgment would be *astonishing*, which is the Hebrew word for *desolate*.

Nothing would be more devastating than for God's chosen people to be removed from that esteemed position in the eyes of God.

The final action that removed them from that status was the stoning of Stephen. The same apostate priesthood that killed Jesus murdered Stephen 3.5 years later. The common thread that connected both Jesus and Stephen's deaths and completed the 70th week was their comments about the Temple. The priesthood had used it for both their wealth and control of the people.

The abomination that brought desolation was the total rejection of Christ by the priesthood of the Jews. This marked the end of the most critical time period in history known as Daniel's 70 weeks and Israel's Old Testament covenant with God. Now there is no difference in God's eyes between the Jew and Gentile.

There is neither Jew nor Greek, there is neither slave nor free, there is neither male nor female; for you are all one in Christ Jesus.

Galatians 3:28

God had given His people so many opportunities to repent and yet they refused to bow their knee to Christ. The clock had run out on God's mercy over the corrupt priesthood and their followers and now only those who remembered the words of Jesus would escape the judgment that was coming, namely the complete destruction of Jerusalem.

I believe the destruction of Jerusalem 36 years later was the result of that action. Nevertheless, in my opinion and according to Edward L. Broomfield[12] the 1,290 days or the final 3.5 years of the 70th week ended on the Day of Atonement in 34 A.D.

Stephen's death was the first death in the name of Jesus after His crucifixion. There had been many persecutions, but this was the beginning of the terror, because Saul of Tarsus was holding the garments of those killing Stephen. Moreover, this ended the time of protection God had provided for the early believers.

This supports my belief, and others as well, that all of the feasts were instituted as physical signposts to direct us to the reality of what transpired **before the foundation of the world.**

Therefore, from the Wave Sheaf or First Fruits Offering on Nissan 18, in 31 A.D. to the Day of Atonement on the 10th day of September, 34 A.D. there are 1,290 days.

---

[12] *https://smoodock45.wordpress.com/2009/11/19/the-70-weeks-prophecy-and-the-1290-days/*

YEAR	31AD	32AD	33AD	34 AD	Total
MONTH					
1st	First Fruits Nissan 18th 12 Days left	30	30	30	
2nd	29	29	29	29	
3rd	30	30	30	30	
4th	29	29	29	29	
5th	30	30	30	30	
6th	29	29	29	29	
7th	30	30	30	Day of Atonement 10th day of the month	
8th	29	29	29		
9th	30	30	30		
10th	29	29	29		
11th	30	30	30		
12th	29	29	29		
13th		29			
Totals	366 days	354 days	383 days	187 days	1290 days

Figure 6

Figure 7

The Jews celebrated the Day of Atonement on the 10th day of the seventh month, in the year 34 A.D. This was the most sacred day in their calendar.

On the very day they were supposed to repent for their transgressions, they were stoning a man filled with faith and the Holy Spirit.

The response by Jesus to Peter prophetically described the length of time God gave Israel to repent.

Then Peter came to Him and said, "Lord, how many times could my brother sin against me and I forgive him? As many as seven times?

*I tell you, not as many as seven, **Jesus said to him, but 70 times seven**.*

Matthew 18:21-22 HCSB

As I said, Stephen's death fulfills the 490 years or 70 weeks prophecy and nothing is more fitting than to end the prophecy on the Day of Atonement 34 A.D. considered by the Jews to be the holiest of all days.

It was revealed to Daniel that all of the kingdoms of this earth would be destroyed by the rock cut without hands.

The last kingdom to fall was the Roman Empire, and as we will discover in Revelation that kingdom was empowered by the Beast, which was the corrupted Jewish Priesthood. They never returned from their evil ways and had become what the dictionary calls apostate.

The word *apostate* originally comes from a Greek word that meant "runaway slave." The people God had rescued from slavery had returned to their original condition as slaves by rejecting God's Laws.

From that point forward all people who want forgiveness for their self-righteousness and murderous ancestry, beginning with Cain, must bow their knee to Jesus, The Christ.

G. BLESSED ARE THOSE WHO REACH 1,335 DAYS

This is stated as the most blessed of the days recorded in Daniel, but why is that?

> *Blessed is he who waits, and comes to the* **one thousand three hundred and thirty-five days.**
>
> *Daniel 12:12 NKJV*

By now it should be obvious that the Bible is written about Christ. God used the Law, especially the Feasts recorded in Leviticus 23, as a guideline or signpost for the people to see Jesus as God's Messiah.

The power of the prophetic is one of the most outstanding features of the scriptures before, during, and after Christ. That is what Jesus is saying in this verse of Revelation.

I am the Alpha and the Omega, the Beginning and the End, says the Lord who Is and who Was and Who is to come, the Almighty.

Revelation 1:8

The fullness of time is contained in that verse. Indeed, the reality of the phrase *before the foundation of the world* is summed up through the realization of the risen Christ.

Jesus of Nazareth and His work was constrained by time. But the risen Christ has no such restraints and has all authority in both the visible and invisible realms. In other words, Jesus completed His assignment within time and in so doing, made all who would call on Him joint heirs with His authority as The Christ.

That means our eyes must be fixed on the spiritual authority He secured while He was both on this planet and in this world. Because most of our problems today are the result of what we believe, not the circumstances we are experiencing.

I am not saying those who "know" the risen Christ will not experience difficult circumstances. But I do believe that if our faith is founded on the resurrected Christ our ultimate outcome will be much different than those whose trust is in man. This is why we must look at the scriptures from a totally different perspective.

The symbols in Daniel and Revelation vividly describe the events surrounding the fulfillment of God's declaration to satan in Genesis. Moreover, if we use tools such as the Feasts and the Intercalary Calendar to calculate the days mentioned in Daniel and Revelation the results are astounding.

Calculating from the feast of Trumpets in 27 A.D., which was both the final Jubilee and the day Jesus read from Isaiah 61, until Pentecost 31 A.D. you arrive at 1,335. The months in the following chart represent the Jewish intercalary calendar. The Jews adopted the Babylonian calendar that follows the moon instead of the sun.

They added a 13th month 3 times every 7 years, which meant some months had 30 days and others 29. In 31 A.D. Pentecost was celebrated the 8th day of the 3rd month. That was 50 days after Nisan 18, when Jesus presented Himself as the Wave Sheaf Offering. Remember, each day was calculated from sundown to sundown or 6 p.m. to 6 p.m.

| Feast of Trumpets 27AD | 1335 Days | Feast of Pentecost 31AD |

Figure 8

YEAR	27AD	28AD	29 AD	30 AD	31 AD	Total
MONTH						
1st		30	30	30	30	
2nd		29	29	29	29	
3rd		30	30	30	Pentecost 8 days left	
4th		29	29	29		
5th		30	30	30		
6th		29	29	29		
7th Feast of the Trumpets	30	30	30	30		
8th	29	29	29	29		
9th	30	30	30	30		
10th	29	29	29	29		
11th	30	30	30	30		
12th	29	29	29	29		
13th		29				
Totals	177 days	383 days	354 days	354 days	67	1335 days

Figure 9

Pentecost was a type of Jubilee after the feast of Passover or First Fruits/Wave Offering. Jesus spent 40 days with His disciples after His resurrection, reestablishing His kingdom and His full authority over the second heaven.

This period of time was necessary to satisfy God's word spoken *before the foundation of the world.*

Moreover, because Jesus fulfilled His assignment God could now send His Holy Spirit to enforce every word Jesus spoke while on the earth.

> *And if anyone hears My words and does not believe, I do not judge him; for I did not come to judge the world but to save the world.*
>
> *He who rejects Me, and does not receive My words, has that which judges him — the word that I have spoken will judge him in the last day.*
>
> *John 12:47-48 NKJV*

The finished work of Christ is the "last day" for those who believe His word and work. The world was saved by what Christ did, but if Man refuses to believe Him that unbelief will judge him.

If Man follows his own ways and beliefs, he will create a world that will be judged by the words of Christ.

The Day of Pentecost ushered in God's kingdom and the New Covenant with all men. Now the earth would be maintained and operated by the Holy Spirit. Remember, Jesus told us that His kingdom is not visible.

Asked by the Pharisees when the kingdom of God would come, He replied to them by saying, The kingdom of God does not come with signs to be observed or with visible display,

Nor will people say, Look! Here [it is]! or, See, [it is] there! For behold, the kingdom of God is within you [in your hearts] and among you [surrounding you].

Luke 17:20-21 AMP

Therefore, if you are waiting on a physical manifestation to reflect your idea of the Kingdom of Heaven, then you haven't understood the words of Christ. Therefore, if you continue to look for spiritual results without changing your mental condition, you will be disappointed. The truth is revealed through the risen Christ. But if we continue to trust doctrines and theologies, our lives will never reflect the reality of what Christ accomplished.

Our minds will begin to comprehend the truth if we use the scriptures to prove God has fulfilled His word through Christ, regardless of the way the physical realm appears.

Think about what was just said! If man continues to use the physical events or circumstances to justify their interpretation of scriptures for a future cataclysmic destruction to occur, NOTHING will ever change.

Our current condition is the result of trusting man's rationalizations constructed from a corrupted mind.

If history has proven anything, it is that men are incapable of rescuing themselves from themselves.

That is why we must celebrate what Jesus accomplished. Otherwise, you will be the self-fulfilling prophet of gloom and doom in your own life.

THE BEAST, THE HARLOT & TEN HORNS

We have been establishing the reality of Christ and His completed work throughout each section of this book. We have offered a different approach to understanding the scriptures by separating the meanings of the words *world* and *earth*.

Moreover, we are constantly reminded that we are spirits that were with our Heavenly Father *before the foundation of the world* outside of time and circumstances. It is important to note that it is only from that position that we can manifest the reality of what Christ accomplished at His Resurrection.

Nevertheless, there are specific scriptures in the Book of Revelation that have created confusion because of our past indoctrinations and lack of knowledge about the historical environment of that time.

Thankfully, there are documents from Flavius Josephus who has shown to be a credible scribe of that time period. His writings will be the source of many of the historical references used in the following chapter.

The Holy Spirit inspired men to write the Bible. The Bible is the written testament between God and man sealed in the blood of Christ Jesus. The true power of that covenant is revealed to those who discover Christ in every prophetic word and symbol of the scriptures.

A close inspection of the prophetic books of the Old Testament reveal much of the language John uses in Revelation. The challenge for us is to understand the horrendous conditions that existed during his time. Most of the historical information is contained within the books of Josephus called "*War of the Jews*".

It is believed that John went to the Isle of Patmos shortly after Herod Agrippa killed his brother James in 43 A.D. Herod was ruling Israel and persecuting the Christians. Life was of no value to the Romans and the anti-Christ spirit of the Jewish priesthood made them complicit in the abominations.

The transition period from the Old to the New Testament was both profound and frightening. It required a complete overthrow of the system.

There is an analogy of this transition written in Ezekiel 3 as well as Revelation 10.

He said, "Mortal man, eat this scroll that I give you; fill your stomach with it." I ate it, and it tasted as sweet as honey.

Then God said, "Mortal man, go to the people of Israel and say to them whatever I tell you to say.

Ezekiel 3:3-4 NKJV

I went to the angel and asked him to give me the little scroll. He said to me, "Take it and eat it; it will turn sour in your stomach, but in your mouth it will be sweet as honey.

I took the little scroll from his hand and ate it, and it tasted sweet as honey in my mouth. But after I swallowed it, it turned sour in my stomach.

Revelation 10:9-10 NKJV

The words of the Old Covenant produced a bitter taste in the bowels of those who once ate the sweetness of God's provision. The protection and blessing God once offered those under the Law had ended. The end of the Old and the beginning of the New was happening just like it was prophesied hundreds of years before.

We have to settle it once and for all that God fulfilled the Law with Jesus in 34 A.D. and the Old Covenant was replaced by the new and better Covenant.

Nevertheless, that transitional period was tumultuous and the accounts of historians such as Flavius Josephus help us to understand such symbols as *7 Heads, 10 Horns, The Beast* and *The Harlot* used in Daniel and Revelation.

Daniel and John both received the same vision concerning the 10 kings and 10 horns. The last kingdom to rule the earth was the Roman Empire. We know the priesthood of the Jews during that time was empowered by satan because they opposed Christ.

Moreover, that spirit worked in conjunction with the Gentile kings that ruled over Jerusalem. History shows there were actually 10 kings that conquered that city.

First let us look at the meaning of the term *beast* and how it applied to the various scriptures in both Daniel and Revelation.

A. THE BEAST

We already defined the term *apostate* from the Greek as a *runaway slave*. The term *beast* was used to describe this apostate condition of Judaism. This is described as the anti-Christ spirit and we know the source of that spirit is satan.

The Bible says the serpent in the Garden of Eden was more cunning than any other beast that God made (Genesis 3:1). Adam's disobedience made him and all his descendants' blood-related to the beast. Sin was passed into all creatures on the earth making it a violent place to live.

Therefore, all those who reject Christ will follow the beast and will be marked the same way Cain was after killing Abel. I believe John is describing those who chose to remove their names from The Book of Life in Revelation 14:9. Jesus defines those in Matthew who received that mark.

A curse is on you, scribes and Pharisees, false ones! For you go about land and sea to get one disciple and, having him, you make him twice as much a son of hell as yourselves.

Matthew 23:15 BBE

The verse in Matthew 23 describes the condition of the priesthood during the day of Jesus and it was this spirit that operated in conjunction with the political systems that produced the picture John wrote about in Revelation.

Most of the Jews who left Babylon followed the Talmud rather than the Torah and populated both in Syria and the Mediterranean. Isaiah is speaking to these people in the following verse.

But come here, You sons of the sorceress,
You offspring of the adulterer and the harlot!

Isaiah 57:3

Daniel described 4 beasts or kingdoms that ruled the earth before the final kingdom, which was Rome. When Jesus came to the earth the land of Israel was already controlled by the anti-Christ spirit, which worked hand and glove with the political system of that time.

The priesthood understood that their power, both spiritually and physically, depended on their being a nation. This gives us insight on why it was so important for the priesthood to remain politically connected with the nations that ruled over them throughout the centuries.

Please remember, I am not attacking flesh and blood or the Jewish people. Jesus of Nazareth was a Jew and was sent to them as their Messiah.

The serpent (or dragon) controlled the political and spiritual powers of that day in the form of Herod and the Priesthood. We who believe the finished work of

Christ are no longer Jew or Greek. Therefore, we are assigned to keep our foot on the neck of the anti-Christ spirit and exalt the risen Christ. Amen!

The picture of the *beast* describes the spiritual condition of a person or society that knows what is right, but would rather be lawless. Nevertheless, every demonic spirit needs a physical entity or body to inhabit in order to manifest. This describes the *beast* written about in Daniel and Revelation.

*This is what he said: **The fourth beast is a fourth kingdom**, which will come on earth, different from all the kingdoms, and it will overcome all the earth, crushing it down and smashing it.*

*And as for the **ten horns, out of this kingdom ten kings** will come to power; and after them another will come up: he will be different from the first ones and will put down three kings.*

Daniel 7:23-24 BBE

*And **the ten horns, which you saw are ten kings**, which still have been given no kingdom; but they are given authority as kings, with the beast, for one hour.*

Revelation 17:12 BBE

*And the dragon stood on the sand of the seashore. Then I saw **a beast** coming up out of the sea, having **ten horns and seven heads**, and on his horns were ten diadems, and on his heads were blasphemous names.*

Revelation 13:1 The Message

*And the angel said to me, "Why do you wonder? I will tell you the **mystery of the woman and of the beast** that carries her, which has the **seven heads and the ten horns**.*

Revelation 17:7 The Message

The anti-Christ spirit forms all religious systems, but the reality that satan had been cast to earth with only a short time left made the Jewish Priesthood his focus.

Read what John says in Revelation 12:

And so be glad, you heavens, and all you that live there! But how terrible for the earth and the sea! For the devil has come down to you, and he is filled with rage, because he knows that he has only a little time left.

Revelation 12:12

The destruction of God´s people was satan's only goal and he knew that if he could corrupt the priesthood, he could kill Jesus. God was never surprised by this nor was Jesus. All of this happened *before the foundation of the world,* but was hidden from the angels, which included satan.

In light of this meaning, let us examine the symbol of the seven heads John saw on the beast.

B. THE 7 HEADS

There are different interpretations concerning these topics in Revelation. But my approach, unlike others, originates from the understanding that Jesus completed His assignment *before the foundation of the world.* That knowledge allows me to connect the history of the time with the Spirit of Truth.

We have defined the beast as the spirit, which controlled the Jewish Priesthood and worked in conjunction with those God called Gentiles.

Jerusalem was conquered by a foreign or Gentile power 7 times in its history. I believe this is the 7-headed beast John witnessed in Revelation 13. It is also important to identify the fulfillment of John's vision in relation to the number 7.

If you read the Book of Revelation you will notice that there are 7 Seals, 7 Trumpets and 7 Bowls. The number seven represents completion and perfection. Each of these events that occurred in "seven", fulfilled the promise of God beginning in Genesis 3 that was to crush the head of satan.

Every kingdom that destroyed Jerusalem drank of the *cup of abomination* spoken of Revelation 17. Therefore, all of the plagues, woes, and destructions cover the history of that city and its atrocities toward God.

1. The first time Jerusalem was destroyed was by Shishak, King of Egypt, who was the first to take it after the death of Solomon.[13]

2. The second time was by Nebuchadnezzar, King of Babylon, who plundered and destroyed both the city and the Temple. This may have been the one referred to as the deadly wound in Revelation 13.[14]

> *One of the heads of the beast seemed to have been fatally wounded, but the wound had healed. The whole earth was amazed and followed the beast.*
>
> *Revelation 13:3*

---

[13] *Josephus: "Antiquities of the Jews," Book VIII, chapter 10, paragraph 3*

[14] *Josephus: "Antiquities of the Jews," Book X, chapter 8, paragraph 5*

We have identified the spirit of anti-Christ as the beast that operated in concert with the Jewish Priesthood and whose sole purpose was to kill Christ and persecute His church.

The Jewish Priesthood, whose corruption began during Solomon's reign, required a Temple to conduct their business, which was based on sacrifices. Nebuchadnezzar destroyed their Temple and took the priesthood captive. This action neutralized the "beast" because satan did not have a body to manifest through.

Therefore, it could be said that the "beast" was killed or mortally wounded as stated in Revelation 13. We know satan was not destroyed at that time, but the spirit of the "beast" that John describes remained dormant until the Temple was rebuilt.

God's ultimate goal was to redeem man and restore His Kingdom, and satan was playing right into the hands of God. All of this was decided and orchestrated *before the foundation of the world.* This whole drama requires a spiritual perception to understand.

Therefore, the whole world worshiped the beast because it kept being brought back to life in the form of the corrupted Jewish Priesthood that seemed to be more interested in serving mammon than heeding God's prophets.

The Jewish Priesthood made the temple a place of abomination. The priests used it as their place of business and control over the people. The mention of destroying the temple by Jesus violently aroused the anti-Christ spirit that had been neutralized once before by Nebuchadnezzar.

3. The third time it was destroyed was by Ptolemy I, a Greek Emperor who controlled Jerusalem through deceit, and took the Temple pretending he wanted to make a sacrifice to God. He entered in peace, but instead he plundered the Temple. This king is the one mentioned in Daniel 11 according to Flavius Josephus in his book *"Antiquities of the Jews"*.[15]

> *Then a mighty king shall arise, who shall rule with great dominion, and do according to his will.*
> *And when he has arisen, his kingdom shall be broken up and divided toward the four winds of heaven, but not among his posterity nor according to his dominion with which he ruled; for his kingdom shall be uprooted, even for others besides these.*

> *Daniel 11:3-4*

4. The fourth was Antiochus IV Epiphanes, described as the King of the North in Daniel 11:21-35. He pillaged and desecrated the

---

[15] *Josephus: "Antiquities of the Jews," Book XII, chapter 1, paragraph 1*

Temple according to Flavius Josephus in *"Antiquities of the Jews"*:[16]

> *And in his place shall arise a vile person, to whom they will not give the honor of royalty; but he shall come in peaceably, and seize the kingdom by intrigue.*
> *With the force of a flood they shall be swept away from before him and be broken, and also the prince of the covenant.*
>
> *And after the league is made with him he shall act deceitfully, for he shall come up and become strong with a small number of people.*
> *He shall enter peaceably, even into the richest places of the province; and he shall do what his fathers have not done, nor his forefathers: he shall disperse among them the plunder, spoil, and riches; and he shall devise his plans against the strongholds, but only for a time.*
>
> *Daniel 11:21-14*

5. The fifth was the Roman Emperor, Pompey the Great. He noted the devotion of the Jews to God and set up priesthood friendly to Rome, thus taking away its traditions and their former dignity, and gave it away for a price.[17]

---

[16] *Josephus: "Antiquities of the Jews," Book XII, chapter 5, paragraph 4*

[17] *Josephus: "Antiquities of the Jews," Book XIV, chapter 4, paragraphs 1 through 5*

6. Herod the Great was the sixth to overthrow Jerusalem. Nevertheless, he did not allow the Temple to be plundered.[18]

7. General Titus of Rome, son of Emperor Vespasian was the seventh and final Gentile to destroy Jerusalem. He conquered Jerusalem and destroyed forever the Temple on the 10th day of the month of Av, 70 A.D. It was not by coincidence, that it was the same day Nebuchadnezzar, King of Babylon, destroyed it during his time.[19]

The verse in Revelation 17 makes sense if we understand the influence of the evil household of Herod and his lineage as an Edomite. We will discuss this later in the book, but I want you to recall he was the king who sent the wise men to find Jesus, in order that he could kill Him.

And they are seven kings: five of them have fallen, and the one is still reigning. The seventh has not yet come, but when he comes he must continue for a short time.

Revelation 17:10 NKJV

The 6th king to destroy the Holy City, Herod the Great, was dead already, but his grandson Herod

---

[18] *Josephus; "Antiquities of the Jews;" Book XV, chapter 1, paragraphs 1 & 2; "Wars of the Jews;" Book I, chapter 18, paragraphs 1 through 3.*

[19] *Josephus: "Wars of the Jews;" Book VI, chapter 4, paragraphs 1 through 8; & chapter x, paragraph 1.*

Agrippa was alive. He was the king who killed James and was operating with the High Priest to destroy the Christians.

Although he was a proconsul, John described him as a king because his authority and territory was the same as his grandfather, Herod The Great.

Therefore, his appearance as a *horn* was because he ruled as both a proconsul and king. The one who was coming and would remain for a short time was Titus, because he destroyed Jerusalem in 70 A.D.

C. THE 10 HORNS

The 7-headed "beast" had 10 horns in Revelation 13. We have discussed the 7 kingdoms that conquered Jerusalem. The last of the 7 heads was Rome. During the time period from 26 A.D. to 70 A.D., 10 Roman procurators ruled Jerusalem. It is these proconsuls that I believe represent the 10 horns. The governors of Judea and Jerusalem, with the exception of Herod Agrippa, were called proconsuls.

However, they had all the power of Herod and perhaps more. The proconsul possessed the authority of *imperium*. In other words, they were autonomous in their authority and were under no obligation to consult higher authorities, including the emperor before making decisions within their provincial command.

These were the various proconsuls and the years they controlled Jerusalem:

1.	Pontius Pilate	26 – 36 A.D.
2.	Marcellus	36 – 38 A.D.
3.	Marullus	38 – 41 A.D.

(There is a 3.5 year gap here where Herod Agrippa I ruled Jerusalem as both the proconsul and king.)

4.	Cuspius Fadus	44 – 46 A.D.
5.	Tiberius Alexander	46 – 48 A.D.
6.	Ventidius Cumanus	48 – 52 A.D.
7.	M. Antonius Felix	52 – 59 A.D.
8.	Porcius Festus	59 – 61 A.D.
9.	Albinus	61 – 65 A.D.
10.	Gessius Florus	65 – 70 A.D.

D. THE HARLOT

*Then one of the seven angels who were carrying the seven bowls came and spoke to me. "Come with me," he said, "and I will show you the doom of **the great Harlot** who sits upon many waters.*

The kings of the earth *have committed fornication with her, and the inhabitants of the earth have been made drunk with the wine of her fornication."*

So he carried me away in the Spirit into a desert, and there I saw a **woman sitting on a scarlet-colored Wild Beast**, *which was covered with names of blasphemy and had seven heads and ten horns.*

The woman was clothed in purple and scarlet, and was brilliantly attired with gold and jewels and pearls. She held in her hand a cup of gold, full of abominations, and she gave filthy indications of her fornication.

Revelation 17:1-4 WEY

Let us reiterate who and what the "beast" represents. As we have said it is both satan and the spirit of anti-Christ, which embodied the Jewish Priesthood during the times of Christ. Hence, the 7-headed beasts were the Gentile kings whose political power joined forces with the *beast's* religious authority to control the region.

All the Gentile kings who joined themselves to the beast and drank of the cup offered by the Harlot were destroyed, including the Roman Empire.

He too shall [have to] drink of the wine of God's indignation and wrath, poured undiluted into the cup of His anger; and he shall be tormented with fire and brimstone in the presence of the holy angels and in the presence of the Lamb.

Revelation 14:10 AMP

Now we turn our attention to the harlot adorned with the same colors and stones used to build the first Tabernacle in the wilderness (Exodus 25-9, 1 Chronicles 29:1-3).

In addition, these stones were used in making the robes and ephod that Aaron and his sons wore as the High Priests. During the 1st century the High Priest was the highest authority among the Jews and as we said they required a geographical and political status. This was achieved by operating in the city of Jerusalem through the vehicle known as the Temple.

And the woman whom you have seen is the great city, which has kingly power over the kings of the earth.

Revelation 17:18 WEY

There are at least 10 references in the Book of Revelation to the "great city." The first and most revealing is found in Revelation 11:8.[20] I wanted to return to this because of its importance.

You might recall that Jesus was prophesying against Jerusalem for killing the prophets and made the following statements.

> *"...that on you may come all the righteous blood shed on the earth, from the blood of righteous Abel to the blood of Zechariah, son of Berechiah, whom you murdered between the temple and the altar.*
>
> *Assuredly, I say to you, all these things will come upon this generation.*
>
> *"O Jerusalem, Jerusalem, the one who kills the prophets and stones those who are sent to her! How often I wanted to gather your children together, as a hen gathers her chicks under her wings, but you were not willing!*
>
> *See! Your house is left to you desolate;"*
>
> *Matthew 23:35-38 NKJV*

---

[20] *The other references are found in the following passages: Revelation 14:8; 16:19; 17:18; 18:10, 16, 18–19, 21*

Obviously, there was no city named Jerusalem when Cain killed Abel. Nevertheless, the spirit of murder resided there because of the bloodshed.

This murderous spirit is called satan who is both the spirit of Jerusalem and the harlot being described in this passage.

The mighty city was broken into three parts, and the cities of the nations fell. And God kept in mind mighty Babylon, to make her drain the cup of His furious wrath and indignation.

Revelation 16:19 AMP

Please notice that Jesus proclaimed that her house (the Temple) would be left desolate. It is clear that the harlot, "Mystery, Babylon the Great, the Mother of Harlots and Abominations of the Earth" was Jerusalem. This city was also described as Sodom and Egypt.

*and their dead bodies will lie in the street of the great city that is **prophetically called Sodom and Egypt**, where also their Lord was crucified.*

Revelation 11:8 TEV

John described the judgment of Jerusalem, which occurred in 70 A.D. Moreover, there is evidence to suggest John wrote Revelation between the years of 43 to 45 A.D. This is because Herod Agrippa, who killed James was ruling Judea and Jerusalem. You recall James was John's brother and it is believed many of the apostles left Jerusalem during his reign.

I think it is false to believe "*Revelation*" was written in 90 A.D. or later. Clement of Alexander, who lived during the end of the 2 A.D. writes that all of the New Testament was completed between the reigns of Tiberius and Nero.[21] They were the Roman Emperors who ruled between 37 and 68 A.D.

It is important to understand that Revelation is the book that reveals the resurrected Christ as King and Judge. That picture should evoke faith inside of each believer, not fear.

Therefore, I believe Revelation should be the first book of the New Testament. This would equip each person with the knowledge of the prophetic word spoken *before the foundation of the world*. In addition, it would aid each believer to understand their role as heirs in Christ as kings and priests.

As a side note, I believe Paul and John crossed paths after his return from Patmos and shortly after Paul wrote his Second letter to Corinthians. In it, he describes John's experience being caught up to the third heaven, which is written in Revelation 4.

---

[21] *http://www.preteristarchive.com/StudyArchive/c/clement-of-alexandria.html*

I know a man in Christ who fourteen years ago — whether in the body I do not know, or whether out of the body I do not know, God knows — such a one was caught up to the third heaven.

2 Corinthians 12:2

Obviously, that is just an opinion, but Paul does say he would not boast about himself, which leads me to believe he was speaking of someone else, otherwise it would sound like he was exalting himself.

There are writings to support that Paul wrote the Second letter to the Corinthians between 50 and 56 A.D.[22] I believe Paul described more of John's experiences in other letters to that Church, but for one reason or another, they are not included in our modern–day Bible.

Nevertheless, the Holy Spirit is well able to provide all of us with more than enough proof of the finished work of Christ *before the foundation of the world.*

---

[22] *http://christianity.about.com/od/newtestamentbooks/a/2-Corinthians.htm*

HEROD AGRIPPA & EDOM

In this chapter, we will discuss the family of Edomites that were in power at the birth of Jesus and after His resurrection. Their bloodline and influence played a significant role in sealing the fate of satan.

In the last chapter, we identified the 10 horns as the 10 kings of the Roman Imperium, which were called *proconsul* or *prefect*. These men ruled over the provinces of Judea and Samaria from 26 A.D. to 70 A.D. However, there is a 42–month period between Marullus and Cuspius Fadus, in which we find the rulership of Herod Agrippa the Great.

Claudius Caesar, Emperor of Rome, made Herod Agrippa, king over all the lands of his grandfather. Agrippa ruled most of Palestine as king for 7 years, but reigned over Jerusalem for only 3.5 years (41 – 44 A.D.).

This makes the verse in Revelation 17:10 much easier to understand.

> *There are also seven kings. Five have fallen, one is, and the other has not yet come. And when he comes, he must continue a short time.*
>
> *Revelation 17:10*

King Herod Agrippa was the grandson of Herod The Great, who was the king who ordered all the children of Bethlehem, less than 2 years of age to be killed.

This decree by King Herod the Great was satan's attempt at revenge for the Angel of Death killing Pharaoh's son in Egypt, (Exodus 12:29-30) and the same spirit that ordered the killing of the babies in Egypt when Moses was born.

Now you start to see the analogy of Jerusalem being named **Egypt**. But what about Sodom, where does this come from? These verses in Ezekiel, referring to Jerusalem, seem to answer that question.

> *"As I live" — the declaration of the Lord God — "your sister **Sodom** and her daughters have not behaved as you and your daughters have.*
>
> *Now this was **the iniquity of your sister Sodom**: she and her daughters had pride,*

plenty of food, and comfortable security, but didn't support the poor and needy.

They were haughty and did detestable things before Me, so I removed them when I saw this...

*...before your own wickedness was uncovered? Now you have become like her, **an object of reproach** and a byword for the daughters of Syria and of **Edom** and for all who are round about them and for the daughters of the Philistines—those round about who despise you.*

You bear the penalty of your lewdness and your [idolatrous] abominations, says the Lord.

Ezekiel 16:48-50 & 16:57-58

There can be little doubt that Ezekiel was describing the future of Jerusalem hundreds of years before John recorded it in Revelation. Later in that same chapter, Ezekiel prophesies that God will remember His Covenant with those who followed His Laws from their "youth." I believe those are the ones John sees asking God "how long must we wait to be avenged" in Revelation 6.

As we have said over and over most of the Jews of Jesus' time were not the offspring of Abraham.

Jesus rebukes them time and time again about their lineage being from their "father" the devil (John 8:44).

The bloodline of the Edomites represented the satanic control that operated during that time. We find in Acts 12:21-23 the premature death of Herod Agrippa I as people were worshiping him. An Angel of the Lord struck him, because he did not give glory to God, and he was eaten by worms and died.

He was stricken with the same disease that killed his grandfather, Herod the Great.[23]

Herod The Great's influence continued through his grandson, Agrippa I, from winter of 41 A.D. to late summer of 44 A.D. Herod and all his descendants were Edomites from the lineage of Esau, who were the enemies of Israel. The Bible prophets Amos, Obadiah and David described God's judgment against them.

According to the book of Jasher, one of the books of the Apocrypha, Edom's connection with Babylon started with Esau's desire to obtain "the valuable garments of Nimrod."

And when Esau saw the mighty men of Nimrod coming at a distance, he fled, and thereby escaped; and Esau took the valuable

---

[23] *Acts 12:21-23; compare Josephus, "Antiquities of the Jews," Book IXX, chapter 8, paragraph 2*

garments of Nimrod, which Nimrod's father had bequeathed to Nimrod, and with which Nimrod prevailed over the whole land, and he ran and concealed them in his house.

Jasher 27:10

Nimrod was both the king and architect of Babylon. He was a dictator and known as a bloody man. His thirst for power and bloodshed re-established the spirit of anti-Christ inherited from the bloodline of Cain, which was the fruit of Adam's sin.

According to the book of Jasher, Esau stole Nimrod's garments that gave him the power to prevail over the land. In essence, Esau took the mantle of the anti-Christ spirit and passed it through all his descendants.

Below is an article on "Essau/Edom" from the Jewish Encyclopedia (1925 edition):

"(In 163 BC) Judas Maccabeus conquered their territory (Edom) for a time. They were again subdued by John Hyrcanus (about 125 BC), by whom they were forced to observe Jewish rites and laws. They were then incorporated with the Jewish nation, and their country was called by the Greeks and Romans, "Idumea." With Antipater began the Idumean dynasty that ruled over Judea till its conquest by the Romans." [24]

---

[24] *http://www.biblebelievers.org.au/bb980916.htm*

The Edomites are neither Israelites nor Jews. They have never been the people of God.

> As it is written, "Jacob I have loved, but Esau I have hated."

> Romans 9:13 NKJV

"So a hundred years before Christ, Judea was inhabited by Edomites and native Israelites who were both followers of Talmudic Judaism, seeming to heal the breach between Jacob and Esau. But the Edomites proved to be a discordant element. And in 37 BC, Herod the Great, an Idumean or Edomite whose wife Mariamne was a Maccabean (Jew), became ruler of Judea. The Pharisees gained ascendancy over the Sadducees, and there were so many Edomites in the population at the time of Christ that a whole land was called Idumea."[25]

This region of the Idumeans was located between Jerusalem and the Dead Sea. The Idumeans were allies of the Sadducees during the wars of the Jews. They profaned the Temple and were responsible for killing many of the Jews inside the entire city. Their hands were just as bloody as the Romans during the destruction of Jerusalem in the year 70 A.D.

---

[25] https://edomsthorn.wordpress.com/2013/01/28/edom-the-story-of-jacob-and-esau-is-not-just-a-stor/

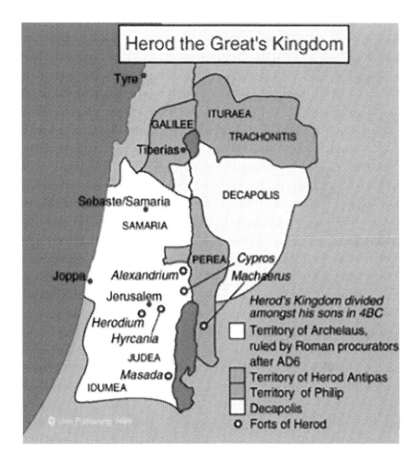

Figure 10

Jacob's name was changed to Israel to extend God's covenant with Abraham and to preserve the bloodline that would fulfill the prophecy of the head bruiser prophesied to the serpent in the garden. But make no mistake, the people Jesus faced in Jerusalem and those who resist Christ are descendants of Esau, not Israel.

The Edomites wore the mantle of Nimrod and perpetuated the systems of Babylon, whose goal has always been to exalt man over God.

Jesus destroyed that system through His Sacrifice and established His Kingdom that rules and reigns today. One of the ways we can identify His Kingdom today is to know what Jesus did *before the foundation of the world*.

His Kingdom is neither threatened nor influenced by Babylon. The reality of that Kingdom in our life is visible through a rebirth by water and the Spirit spoken about by Jesus in John 3. This spiritual truth manifested outside of time *before the foundation of the world*.

THE HORN WITH
EYES & MOUTH

I was watching the horns with care, and I saw another coming up among them, a little one, before which three of the first horns were pulled up by the roots: and there were eyes like a man's eyes in this horn, and a mouth saying great things.

Daniel 7:8 BBE

Perhaps, one of the strangest parts of the prophecy revealed to both Daniel and John is related to the description of this horn with the eyes and mouth. Both describe this horn as having more authority than the others and with the ability to wage war against God's chosen people.

We have described the Edomite control and hatred of the Jews during that time. A closer inspection of the Priesthood, namely Annas will expose some of the mystery behind the language used by John.

The description of the beast in Revelation 13 is John's way of illustrating Herod Agrippa's role as both the ruler over Jerusalem and one of the 7 heads of the beast.[26]

> *And the beast was given the power of speech, uttering boastful and blasphemous words, and he was given freedom to exert his authority and to exercise his will during forty-two months (three and a half years).*
>
> *And he opened his mouth to speak slanders against God, blaspheming His name and His abode, [even vilifying] those who live in heaven.*
>
> *He was further permitted to wage war on God's holy people (the saints) and to overcome them. And power was given him to extend his authority over every tribe and people and tongue and nation,*
>
> *And all the inhabitants of the earth will fall down in adoration and pay him homage, everyone whose name has not been recorded in the Book of Life of the Lamb that was slain* **from the foundation of the world**.
>
> *Revelation 13:5-8 AMP*

---

[26] *Josephus; "Antiquities of the Jews;" Book XV, chapter 1, paragraphs 1 & 2; "Wars of the Jews;" Book I, chapter 18, paragraphs 1 through 3.*

Herod Agrippa, in conjunction with the priesthood, whose headship consisted of Annas and Caiaphas, ordered the beheading of John's brother, James.

It was during that period Herod Agrippa was terrorizing the followers of Christ in Jerusalem and I believe contributed to John going to Patmos. In my opinion, the early church was familiar with the horrors of most of the Jewish priesthood and Roman tyranny.

I believe *the little horn* was Herod Agrippa and the eyes and mouth speaking blasphemous things against God was his false prophet Annas the priest. Annas was both the power and the father-in-law of Caiaphas, the high priest, who was responsible for the crucifixion of Jesus. He was the one described in Revelation 13 as a Lamb that spoke like a dragon. He received his power from satan or *the beast* whose head was Herod Agrippa.

> *And about the ten horns on his head and the other which came up, causing the fall of three; that horn which had eyes, and a mouth saying great things, which seemed to be greater than the other horns.*

> *And I saw how that horn made war on the saints and overcame them,*

> *Daniel 7:20-21 BBE*

Annas is *the False Prophet* (Revelation 13:11-18; 16:13; 19:20; 20:10) and *the Man of Sin* (2 Thessalonians 2:3) to whom the New Testament refers. Annas was removed as High Priest by Rome, but according to Jewish law, a High Priest is like a Judge on the Supreme Court that remains until their death.

He made it his personal vendetta not only to crucify Jesus, but also to hunt down and persecute Jews who believed the message of Jesus all over Judea and the Roman Empire.

His madness lasted for a 3.5 year period in conjunction with the support and headship of Herod Agrippa. History and the Scriptures describe the Apostles leaving Jerusalem and probably all of Palestine for at least as long as Agrippa ruled.[27]

It is interesting to note that Joseph and Mary had to flee Bethlehem with Jesus when Herod's grandfather was king. The hatred of the Edomites was the fuel God used to assure His plan to sacrifice His Son and redeem man would come to pass.

There are many who read the Book of Revelation, which is called the "Revelation of Jesus Christ" and determine that it is about a planet wide tribulation and second coming of Jesus during their lifetimes.

---

[27] *https://smoodock45.wordpress.com/2011/07/24/the-mouth-of-the-beast/*

It is my prayer that the Holy Spirit will open your heart to the reality of what Jesus finished, *before the foundation of the world,* and as a new beginning for you to conduct your own search for the risen Christ.

Nevertheless, my opinion along with others, support the belief that the events described in Paul's letters and John's revelations are directly related to the 1st century A.D. and describe the horrendous judgments of Jerusalem and the anti-Christ spirit.

Moreover, I fully recommend that you read my wife's book *"The End of an Era"* to receive greater understanding of that time and history in your pursuit of The Truth.

My prayer is for the Holy Spirit to awaken your spirit to your condition *before the foundation of the world* when you witnessed Christ fulfill His assignment.

I want to remind you of this, our world is constructed from our ideas, thoughts and beliefs. The world Jesus died for and received for His sacrifice was the world that originated before Adam. This was the dimension of consciousness that was before the contamination and corruption of sin.

The power of choice is the two-edged sword that opens our eyes to our condition in the natural or His finished work in the Spirit. Jesus is that finished work; but you knew that *before the foundation of the world.* The good news is, Jesus became our form as the Last Adam to redeem our bloodline and restore our sight. The truth of what Jesus fulfilled will require eternity to comprehend. These books are but tools in your search.

And made them kings and priests to our God, and they reign on earth.
Revelation 5:10

III. SUMMARY

The finished works of God are highlighted in both Daniel and Revelation. Daniel sets the stage for the final act between satan and God. It was both the best and worst of times on planet earth. The best because satan was defeated and cast out of heaven. It was the worst of times because the transition between the Old and New Testaments required the martyrdom of God's disciples and the death of hundreds of thousands of Jews.

The description of that tumultuous time is illustrated in Revelation and spoken about in 2 Peter 3:10. The end of the reign of satan in the heavens and the destruction of his works on the earth (1 John 3:8).

Therefore, two of the most important books that confirm the proclamation God made to satan in Genesis are Daniel and Revelation. If we make that a foundational piece in our reading of the scriptures, the Bible is a much easier book to comprehend. Below are highlights from the scriptures and from this book that will serve as a tool in your future studies.

Remember, this is not another theology or doctrine.

- Daniel describes the 4 kingdoms that ruled the earth in the form of a statue. (Daniel 2:32-47) This statue is the heart and soul of both Daniel and Revelation as it pertains to the various kings and kingdoms that operated from Babylon to Rome.

- Beginning in Daniel Chapter 7, God begins to reveal His master plan that will ultimately usher in Christ and establish God's kingdom on the earth once again.

- Daniel Chapter 8 reveals the various kingdom battles between the King of Greece, Darius the Mede, Alexander the Great and Antiochus Epiphanes that play the role in the 7-headed beast seen by John in Revelation.

- Daniel Chapter 9 establishes the physical timeline that allotted Israel to repent and accept the coming Messiah, which is described by the 70-weeks spoken of in Daniel 9:24-27.

- I believe in Daniel 10:6, Jesus speaks to Daniel because the same thing happens to the people around Daniel that happened to Paul on the road to damascus.

- Chapters 11 and 12 of Daniel explain in detail the kings that arise and the various wars culminating in the capture or destruction of Jerusalem until it's final destruction by Titus in 70 A.D.

- Daniel 12:4 *And thou, O Daniel, hide the things, and seal the book till the time of the end, many do go to and fro, and knowledge is multiplied.*

- This is the book that God is holding in His hand in Revelation. Jesus is the only one who can open it. All of the horrors described in the book of Revelation describe the wars waged against the various Jewish nations.[28]

- The Book of Revelation concentrates on the final kingdom to rule the earth in conjunction with the corrupt priesthood of Israel. The 7th head of the beast and 10 horns represents this picture.

---

[28] *After the captivity in Babylon, the Jews migrated to various parts of central Asia and Europe, forming what they called the Jewish Nations, or Kingdoms. These are the ones that gathered on the day of Pentecost and heard their languages been spoken. They had gone to Jerusalem for the celebration of the Jewish feasts.*

- The beast is the anti-Christ spirit and operated through the priesthood of Israel in conjunction with the Edomite king Herod Agrippa I. That spirit is still alive on the earth today and is visible in religions and persons who resist Christ.

- It is my belief, and supported by Edward Broomfield, that the priesthood of Annas and Caiaphas are the false prophets in John's vision.

- *Power was given him to wage war against the saints* (according to Revelation 13:7 and similarly in Daniel 7:21, 25; 8:24-25). Annas was possessed by satan to destroy God's saints. He led the assault against the stoning of Stephen.

- He instigated the deaths of James the apostle, and the killing of James, the Lord's brother.

- There is a common theme in the letters of James, Peter, John, and Jude alerting the church against false teachers (anti-christs) who were dividing the flock. This is the 42 months mentioned in Revelation 13:5 and the time, times and half a time (3.5 years) mentioned in Daniel 7:25.

- Annas was killed with a sword at the outbreak of the war with Rome at the hand of one of the rebels [Josephus: Wars 2.17.1-10].

If any man sends others into prison, into prison he will go: if any man puts to death with the sword, with the sword will he be put to death. Here is the quiet strength and the faith of the saints.

Revelation 13:10

All too often we forget that our life as physical beings on the earth operates in a linear fashion. In other words, we have a beginning and end as human beings. However, our true nature is spiritual and eternal, which is not limited by time or our physical senses. The Bible is written in the physical realm and uses time to confirm the spiritual reality of the prophetic frequency released in this dimension.

It was necessary for God to send Gabriel to connect the heavenly frequency of God's Word to the physical realm regarding what He spoke to satan in the Garden.

His Word was fulfilled *before the foundation of the world* and assured that everything that was and is and was to come would be completed.

CONCLUSION

*Do you not believe that I am in the Father,
and the Father in Me? The words that I speak
to you I do not speak on My own authority; but
the Father who dwells in Me does the works.*

John 14:10 NKJV

The Bible is the testimony of Christ's victory in
reconciling God's prize creation *Man*, back to His
Father. In order to fulfill that assignment, Jesus had
to rely totally on The Father. In other words, God was
Jesus and Jesus was God, there was no difference
between them. Jesus of Nazareth was the physical
vessel God needed to destroy the works of satan,
because Adam had made covenant with satan by
trusting him over God.

Therefore, *The Last Adam* (Jesus) needed to
physically die to destroy that covenant, but His
resurrection assured all who would believe in Him
victory over the voices of fear, doubt and unbelief.

If Jesus of Nazareth submitted His vessel to God, in order for God to work through Him and destroy the works of satan — how much greater should our works be now that satan has been cast out, from the place of his power?

> *Most assuredly I tell you, he who believes in me, the works that I do, he will do also; and greater works than these will he do; because I am going to my Father.*

> *John 14:12 WEB*

The greater works begin by first understanding the complete victory over satan and his kingdom. The works of satan are the same today as it was during the times of Jesus. They operate according to **unbelief**. Herein, lies the heart of the problem with the belief that teaches satan will destroy the earth, in order for Jesus to return to save Jerusalem.

If we refuse to believe that God destroyed satan's control over unbelief, then we make God a liar and invoke the defeated devil over your life.

This is why it is so important for you to study the scriptures from the position of victory and not from a theology that creates fear like that of a future destruction of the earth.

We must conclude that Jesus left nothing undone that would require Him to return to finish what He gave us the authority to do. The question one should be asking is not "when is He returning" — but "what is my responsibility now that I know the truth?"

Let me suggest a couple of things that you may want to consider, to help you answer my last question. If you recall, it was the priesthood that satan controlled. satan knows the power of God, but he also understood the weakness of man, which was and is to rely on his senses for solutions.

Regardless of your belief about the location of satan today, it must be completely understood that you have authority over him. That being settled now, you are left with a decision to make about your responsibility as a king and priest on the earth.

Jesus made it perfectly clear, it was to our advantage for Him to leave the earth in order to release the Holy Spirit. We know that, but do we understand His unlimited power to change our consciousness?

Science has measured the average time human beings are conscious or aware of what they are thinking about is less than 10 seconds a minute. Unless we can consciously observe the presence of God more than 10 seconds a minute, we will be unable to manifest our limitless power through faith.

God has given us a priesthood that cannot be corrupted, but is equipped to offer help to those who are willing to pay the price. This priesthood is called *the Priesthood of Melchizedek*. Jesus said something very interesting:

> **Your father Abraham rejoiced to see my day. He saw it, and was glad.**
>
> **John 8:56 WEB**

The most powerful tool to change our mental condition and consciousness is to submit to *the Priesthood of Melchizedek*. My next book in this series will be about that order and the power it will make in society.

I trust this book and all future books will provoke you to ask the Holy Spirit to be your guide. Like the early disciples of Berea, ask the Holy Spirit to be your Teacher.

Remember, Jesus said God would not give us a stone if we ask for bread. Trust Him for your daily bread and watch your life change.

Until next time, peace and grace be multiplied to you and yours.

The End

For further study, we recommend this book

by Dr. Ana Mendez Ferrell

The End Of An Era

Rediscovering A Hidden History

Rediscover a hidden history that will redefine your understanding about the "End of The World" and Biblical prophecy. This book will change your life!

www.voiceofthelight.com

Participate in our courses live and

On Demand

If you enjoyed reading this book, we also recommend

The Last Adam

Who Has Bewitched You?

Immersed In Him

Quantum Fasting

www.voiceofthelight.com

Watch us on Frequencies of Glory TV
and follow us on Facebook

www.frequenciesofglorytv.com

www.facebook.com/EmersonFerrell
www.facebook.com/VoiceoftheLight

Contact our ministry at:

Voice of The Light Ministries
P.O. Box 3418
Ponte Vedra, FL. 32004
USA
904-834-2447

www.voiceofthelight.com